BLACK EAGLES

African Americans
in Aviation

BLACK EAGLES

African Americans in Aviation

JIM HASKINS

SCHOLASTIC INC.

NEW YORK

Published by Scholastic Inc.
SCHOLASTIC HARDCOVER is a registered trademark of Scholastic Inc.

Library of Congress Cataloging-in-Publication Data

Haskins, James, 1941–
    Black Eagles : African Americans in aviation / by Jim
Haskins.
        p.   cm.
    Includes bibliographical references (p.   ) and index.
    1. Afro-Americans in aeronautics — United States —
Juvenile literature.   I. Title.
TL553.H35   1995
629.13'08996073 — dc20   94-18623
                                                       CIP
                                                        AC

                    ISBN 0-590-45912-0

12 11 10 9 8 7 6 5 4 3 2 1   5 6 7 8 9/9 0/0
                Printed in the U.S.A.   37
        First Scholastic printing, February 1995

ACKNOWLEDGEMENTS

I am grateful to Kathy Benson, Deborah C. Brudno,
Thomas N. Celentano, and Ann Kalkhoff for their help.
Special thanks to my editor, Ann Reit,
for her patience and support.

To Johnny Ray Haskins, Jr.

CONTENTS

BLACK EAGLES

African Americans
in Aviation

1

THE PIONEERS

FOR as long as humans have been on earth, they have dreamed of being able to take wing and fly like birds above the clouds. Many myths and folktales include stories of people flying. African-American folklore is especially rich in stories and songs about people flying, such as this one:

> *Sugarman done fly away*
> *Sugarman done gone*
> *Sugarman cut across the sky*
> *Sugarman gone home . . .*

Folklore from other cultures is also filled with tales of people flying.

But humans don't have wings; and after a while people realized that if they were to fly other than in their imaginations they would have to build flying machines. The Italian artist, musician, engineer, and scientist Leonardo da Vinci, who lived from 1452 to 1519, studied bird flight and made drawings of a flying machine that survive in his notebooks today. Many less famous men and women may also have made such drawings and even built models.

The first successful flying machines were those that did not try to copy bird flight. They were hot-air balloons, which people had designed in the thirteenth century, even before the time of Leonardo da Vinci. The first hot-air balloons were actually built in France in 1783 by the brothers Joseph Michael and Jacques Étienne Montgolfier. In 1783, they managed to cause a balloon, 100 feet in diameter, made of linen filled with heated air, to rise 6,000 feet above the ground.

In 1853, Sir George Cayley, an Englishman, successfully tested a glider of his own design. It was an aircraft without an engine, because at that time no one had yet managed to build an engine that was both powerful and light. Cayley's glider was the result of years of investigation into such things as wing design, steering rudders, and vertical tail surfaces. Because of his discoveries, Cayley is recognized as the founder of aerodynamics.

Aerodynamics is the study of gases in motion. Air is a gas, and the most important gas used in flight and in the design of aircraft. From the time of Sir George Cayley in the middle 1800s to the time of the Wright brothers in the early 1900s, many people tried and failed to build aircraft that could fly.

The introduction of the automobile engine in the late nineteenth century proved a turning point in the history of human flight. Orville and Wilbur Wright, two Americans in their thirties, were finally able to produce an airplane with two propellers driven by a gasoline motor. At Kitty Hawk,

The only photograph of man's first flight; Orville Wright is in the plane and Wilbur Wright is running at the side.

North Carolina, on December 17, 1903, the Wrights actually succeeded in keeping their craft in the air for twelve seconds; and later attempts on the same day lasted longer.

In those early days, there was still much experimentation in the building of aircraft. The most common types were made of steel and wood, with fabric-covered firm wings. But some models had wings that could flap like a bird's. Each aircraft designer aimed for lighter and stronger models and faster, more powerful engines.

The building and flying of aircraft remained a hobby for scientists, inventors, and other private citizens until the outbreak of World War I in Europe in 1914. Seeing the potential uses for airplanes in war, many governments began to produce the craft for military use. By the time the United States entered World War I in 1917, the United States Army Air Service had been founded.

At that time, the United States military was segregated. Blacks could serve as cooks and laundrymen, could build fortifications and clean latrines (field bathrooms); but they could not serve in combat. There was no separate U.S. Air Force at the time—military aviation was under the control of the Army—but if it had existed it would not have admitted blacks. The white powers-that-be who did not consider blacks fit for ground or naval combat duty certainly could not imagine them ever being fighter pilots. But just as young whites dreamed of taking to the air in flying machines, so did young blacks. And one African American, Eugene Bullard, was determined to be a pilot in World War I.

Eugene Jacques Bullard was born in Columbus, Georgia, in 1894. He ran away from home when he was a boy and stowed away on a ship to Scotland. There he became a welterweight prizefighter and boxed in England, France, and North Africa.

Bullard was 20 years old when World War I began in Europe. He enlisted in the French Foreign Legion, a volunteer armed force composed primarily of non-Frenchmen. He suffered the first of four war wounds at the battle of Verdun in France early in the war. While recovering from that first wound, Bullard transferred to the French flying corps. Whether he got his flight training there or had been trained earlier is not known. His job was to pilot scout and fighter planes.

Other American pilots had gone to France during the war, and by 1916 the French government had decided to form a branch of its air service called *Escadrille Américaine* (American Squadron). In De-

Pioneer aviator Eugene Bullard, who fought with the French in World War I.

cember 1916 the name was changed to the Lafayette Escadrille, after the Marquis de Lafayette, the French general and statesman who had helped George Washington and his colonial army fight the British during the American Revolution. Bullard served briefly with the unit. By the time the war ended in 1918, he had proved himself so valuable to the French cause that he was awarded several medals, including the French Legion of Honor and the *Croix de Guerre* (War Cross), the highest honor given by the French military.

American flyers in the volunteer Lafayette Escadrille, in France, pictured here with their lion cub mascot.

After the war, in January 1918, the Lafayette Escadrille was reorganized in the United States Army as the 103rd Pursuit Squadron. But it was only for the white pilots who had served the French government. Bullard had little interest in returning to the United States anyway, for in Europe he had found a respect and freedom from discrimination that he had never experienced in his native land. He remained in France, working as a band leader and then owning two restaurants on the Left Bank of Paris (the area where intellectuals and the small population of blacks from Guadeloupe and other French colonies lived). He named one of the restaurants L'Escadrille after the flying unit in which he had served during World War I. He also ran a gymnasium for prizefighters for a time.

Bricktop, born Ada Beatrice Queen Victoria Louise Virginia Smith, an African-American entertainer, arrived in Paris in 1924 to perform at Le Grand Duc, where Bullard was the manager. She was impressed by this tall, handsome African American who was so self-assured. Just days after her arrival, she suffered acute appendicitis. She began feeling the pain on a Friday evening, and Bullard took her to a doctor. Although the doctor said she should be operated on immediately, he also said it wouldn't be possible to schedule the oper-

Bricktop entertaining in Paris.

ation until Monday. She recalled in her autobiography, *Bricktop*, "Gene lost his temper. He raised the roof, hollering that as a flyer he'd done so much for France and now he wanted something done for his countrywoman. He ended up in tears. I wish I could have enjoyed the performance more. The doctor gave in and scheduled the operation for Sunday."

When Bricktop married Peter DuConge, a saxophonist from New Orleans, in 1929, Eugene Bullard served as best man, guiding the couple through the French marriage ceremony and prompting them when to say *Oui* (yes, I do). Bullard, too, said *Oui* when he married a Frenchwoman.

After World War II began in Europe, Bullard used his position as a nightclub owner and manager to spy for the French Underground. He also joined the French Army and was severely wounded at Orléans in France. By the fall of 1939, Hitler's German forces threatened France, and the American consulate in Paris was warning all American citizens to leave France. Of the Americans in France, those in greatest danger were African Americans, for an important part of Nazi Germany's campaign for world domination was "racial purity" and hatred of Jews, Gypsies, and blacks. "It was a terrible situation, heartbreaking in a lot of cases," recalled Bricktop, who had come to feel that Paris was her home. "The most tragic were those affecting Americans who had married Frenchwomen. There were children to consider. Gene Bullard got caught in this bind. He had a French wife, and he finally had to leave her. It was either that or go to a concentration camp."

Smuggled out of France by American friends, as Bricktop also was, Bullard returned to the United

States in 1940 and settled in the East Harlem section of New York City. Among other jobs, he operated an elevator in the RCA Building. In 1954, the government of France invited him to relight the flame of the Tomb of the Unknown Soldier in Paris. But aside from that brief moment of renewed fame, Bullard remained relatively unknown in his native country. He died in October 1961 at the age of 67.

By the time Bricktop had arrived in Paris in 1924, Americans had made great strides in the science of manned flight. In fact, spurred in large measure by the public awareness of manned flight during the First World War, the 1920s and 1930s were a time of unprecedented advances in aircraft design and use. They were also a time when more and more would-be flyers were able to acquire airplanes of their own, for there were many surplus aircraft left over from the war. This was especially so in California, which during the war had become a center for the production of military aircraft.

Public interest in flying was kept alive by public exhibitions. There was as yet no commercial airline industry; so people who wished to make their livings as flyers had to go into the air-circus business, appearing at county fairs, staging air shows that featured daring stunts, and giving brave people in the audience short rides in the airplanes. The growing movie industry, which also was centered more and more in California, especially in the part of Los Angeles called Hollywood, was another spur to the popularity of flying. Many movies about flying were produced, almost all featuring white flyers, of course. But there was also a black movie industry, which produced films for black audiences that were called "race films." The 1926 film *The Flying Ace* featured an all-black cast, lots of flying, and an exciting midair battle in which two black pilots, the hero and the villain, fight over a beautiful black woman.

The model for the flying ace in the film might well have been Hubert Fauntleroy Julian, a native of Trinidad who saw an airplane for the first time in his hometown of Port of Spain in 1911, when he was 17 years old. The young Julian was impressed not only with the plane but also with the pilot's dress and self-assured manner; and the memory stayed with him.

The child of a well-to-do family, Julian was attending school in England when war clouds began to thicken over Europe. In 1914, he went to Canada to continue his education and there, in Montreal, Quebec, he began to hang around at the city's airfield, which coincidentally was called St. Hubert. He took his first ride in an airplane in 1919 with a

COLONEL HUBERT JULIAN, WORLD'S FOREMOST PIONEER NEGRO AVIATOR AND A CONTESTANT FOR THE WORLD'S LONG DISTANCE NON-STOP RECORD

Colonel Hubert Julian.

13

World War I hero named Billy Bishop and was so impressed by the experience that he learned to fly himself. He became one of the earliest black flyers to have a pilot's license.

Hubert Julian moved to New York City in 1921 and soon became well known as the Black Eagle, a daring flyer and showman who was always thinking up new stunts. In 1923, he parachuted from an airplane down onto West 139th Street in Harlem, causing a traffic jam and earning himself a ticket from the police.

By the following year, he had acquired his own war-surplus airplane, which he named *Ethiopia I*, after the nation of Ethiopia in Africa. He announced that he would become the first person to fly solo across the Atlantic Ocean, but his plane never left New York City. Instead, it nosedived into Flushing Bay shortly after takeoff.

After he had recovered from the accident, Julian returned to his barnstorming and stunt-flying. Using the title "Black Eagle of Harlem," he crisscrossed the United States, appearing in whatever air shows he could finance. He was a master at self-promotion and was probably the best known African-American flyer of the time.

His fame even reached Ethiopia, whose emperor, Haile Selassie, invited him to organize an air force for the nation. Julian arrived in Ethiopia in 1930 with big plans. But he found that Ethiopia, with few good planes, was ill-equipped to start an air force. Although he and an African-American pilot from Chicago named John Robinson attempted to build an Ethiopian air force, they had not succeeded by the time Italy, under Italian dictator Benito Mussolini, invaded Ethiopia in 1935 and they were forced to leave.

Julian often spoke of trying again to make a solo flight across the Atlantic, but he never found the financial backing to make his dream possible. Through his stunts and air-show appearances, however, he kept black aviation alive.

Although black aviators like Hubert Julian dreamed of history-making feats like a solo transatlantic flight, it was white aviation pioneers such as Charles Lindbergh (1902-1974) and Amelia Earhart (1897-1937) who were able to raise the money to score the major "firsts" in American aviation.

Lindbergh made the first transatlantic flight, from New York to Paris, in 1927. The following year, Earhart became the first woman to make a solo flight across the Atlantic.

All the publicity surrounding these milestones in aviation history attracted more Americans to flying schools that were opening in various parts of the country, and to the flying clubs that proliferated throughout the nation. But blacks were notably absent from all this excitement and activity. Many white flying *clubs* in the North were willing to admit black flyers, because aviators were a small and close group who respected each other; but no white flying *schools* would do so. Blacks, discouraged by the entire social structure of the nation from even presuming to be flyers, were forced to be content with only dreaming about piloting aircraft.

There were a few exceptions, however. An important event that occurred in the early 1920s was the pilot's license granted to Bessie Coleman, the first African-American woman flyer (or aviatrix, as women flyers were called then to distinguish them from male aviators).

2

BESSIE COLEMAN

BESSIE Coleman was born on January 26, 1892, in Atlanta, Texas, a town near where the borders of Texas, Arkansas, and Louisiana meet. The town had been named by people who had migrated from Georgia to build the Texas and Pacific Railroad. Missing home, they had named it after the capital city of Georgia.

Coleman's mother, Susan, was African American and the child of some of those immigrants from Georgia. Coleman's father, George, was one-quarter African American and three-quarters Native American, and considered himself an American Indian. Although neither he nor his wife could read or write, they were hard-working people who wanted to make a comfortable life for themselves and their family of three girls—Lillah, Alberta, and Bessie—and three boys—Walter, Isaiah, and John. George Coleman worked as a day laborer and man-

17

aged to save enough money to buy a small plot of land in Waxahachie, south of the city of Dallas. The family moved there when Bessie was two years old. Three more girls were born in Waxahachie: Elois in 1894, Nilus in 1896, and Georgia in 1898.

When she was six, Coleman started school in a one-room wooden building four miles from home. She walked there and back every day. As with other things in Texas, the school was segregated. One teacher taught pupils of all ages with the aid of few books, paper, or pencils. Coleman didn't realize how inadequate the school was compared to white schools in the area. She loved school and soon proved herself especially good in math.

But her father was painfully aware of the segregation in Texas, which denied him the opportunity to vote, to ride in the same railroad car as whites, or to get a better job. He was subjected to this segregation more because he was Native American than black, and so he decided that he and his family could find a better life in Oklahama, where his father had been born. There, in Indian territory, he and his family would enjoy the full rights of citizens.

But Susan Coleman had no interest in moving to Indian territory. In spite of the fact that there were very few black single mothers and that she would have to be the sole support of her family, she refused to accompany her husband. George Coleman left, and the family split up.

Susan Coleman got a job as a cook-housekeeper for Mr. and Mrs. Jones, a local white couple. The five older children had left home by then, so Bessie had to stay home with her three little sisters and miss weeks and weeks of the school she loved. But her mother helped to teach her by having her read to the family from the Bible every night; and Susan Coleman got books from the wagon library that passed through town every few months. She also observed the manners and the way of speaking of her educated white employers and taught her children to emulate them.

At cotton-picking time, all the Coleman children who could help out joined the other black children in the area in the cotton fields. The schools for black children were closed; Susan Coleman was excused from her work at the Jones's; and the whole family grabbed at the chance to make some money. Bessie, however, was the only one in the family who could weigh the full sacks of cotton for payment and make sure the foreman was not cheating them.

Coleman's abilities in reading and math, as well as her awareness that she was successfully carrying out the responsibilities of an adult by taking care of the Coleman home and younger children, gave her great self-confidence. At a very young age, she decided she wanted to go to college, and so she studied hard at school whenever she was able to go, and finished all eight grades at the one-room school for blacks. Then, with her mother's encouragement, she began taking in laundry in order to earn money to continue her education.

In 1910, at the age of eighteen, Coleman enrolled at the Colored Agricultural and Normal University in Langston, Oklahoma. It was a vocational program that offered a preparatory school for students who could not meet the full entrance requirements. Coleman's limited and frequently interrupted schooling did not qualify her for anything but the preparatory school, where she was placed in the sixth grade.

Coleman loved being at the school and made many friends. Unfortunately, her money ran out after she had completed one term. Still, she had managed to get farther in school than any other black—and most whites—in Waxahachie.

Back home, Coleman returned to the laundry business and dreamed of a better life. In 1915, when she was twenty-three years old, she traveled north to Chicago in the segregated railroad car of the Rock Island Line to join her brothers Walter and John. Chicago at that time was a magnet for blacks from

A later picture of Bessie Coleman, also called "Brave Bessie" for her flying stunts.

the South and Southwest; between 1910 and 1920 the city's black population doubled, as African Americans escaped the segregation of the South and looked for greater opportunities in the northern cities.

At that time, the only employment opportunities for untrained black women in Chicago were as domestics. Coleman had had enough of domestic work as a laundress. She decided to become a manicurist. After learning the manicure trade, she went to work in a barber shop. Beautiful and intelligent, she was soon a favorite among the customers, whose tips, coupled with her earnings, enabled her to move out of her brothers' house and get her own apartment. Her success caused her mother and two of her sisters to move to Chicago as well, her sisters arriving with their children and without their husbands. They stayed with Bessie or with Walter and John until they found work.

Coleman herself had married about a year before the arrival of her mother and sisters. But she never lived with Claude Glenn, a family friend who was fourteen years her senior. She also never discussed her marriage, even with her family; and the only evidence of it is a license issued in December 1916.

Three months after Coleman's marriage, the

United States declared war on Germany and entered World War I. It was during this war that airplanes began to be used for something more than recreation, and Bessie Coleman became an avid reader of reports about airplanes and flying in the conflict. Both Walter and John were members of the all-black Eighth Army National Guard, and both served in France. Many African Americans served bravely in the war, then returned to civilian life to face the same discrimination and segregation as before. In fact, black veterans' expectations that they deserved fairer treatment from a grateful nation only served to worsen race relations.

Another factor that made things tenser was the change in the employment situation for blacks in northern cities during the war. With so many white men enlisting in the armed services, jobs opened up, and blacks filled them. White veterans returned to find that blacks had taken their jobs. In Chicago, many of those jobs were in the meat-packing industry. The city's black population had tripled in just a year and a half. Chicago experienced its worst race riot in the summer of 1919, not long after the war ended. A black youth on a homemade raft drifted into a swimming area of Lake Michigan used by whites. Some whites threw stones at him, and he drowned. Soon, blacks and whites were fighting in the streets. Four days later, the National Guard was called in to restore order. Thirty-eight people (mostly blacks) died, 537 were injured, and more than 1,000 were left homeless.

For both John and Walter Coleman, their war experiences, especially their experiences in France where there was little antiblack feeling, were central to their lives. John, especially, loved to tell stories about his time in France and about the French women. He constantly marveled that some even flew airplanes.

The first French woman to become a licensed female pilot was Baroness Raymonde de La Roche in 1909. Two years later, Harriet Quimby became the first American woman to do so. People in the United States did not approve of female pilots, and Quimby had been forced to go to France to achieve her goal. She earned her pilot's license from the Fédération Aéronautique Internationale (International Aeronautical Federation) on August 2, 1911. Sadly, Quimby died less than a year later when her plane crashed into Dorchester Bay in Boston as she was preparing for an air show.

One day, Bessie's brother John walked into the barber shop where she worked and started on his favorite theme, the superiority of French women. "You nigger women ain't never goin' to fly," he told his sister laughingly. "Not like those women I saw in France."

Coleman laughed back. "That's it!" she said. "You just called it for me." What she meant was that her brother had just given her a life's calling, or purpose. But it is doubtful that her choice was that sudden or that simple. For most of her life, Bessie Coleman had wanted to be someone special. Over time, the thought had begun to occur to her that no one could be more special than a *black* American *woman* pilot. That would be a first!

The initial step in becoming the first black American woman pilot was to find someone to teach her. Coleman approached several fliers, but all of them turned her down. All were white; there were no black fliers in the Chicago area at that time. Whether they refused her because she was black or because she was a woman is not known; the reason is probably a combination of both.

Coleman had no intention of giving up. Through her job, she had met many influential people in Chicago's black community. She confided her dreams to anyone who would listen and eventually caught the attention of Robert Abbott, the editor and publisher of the highly influential black newspaper, the *Chicago Defender*. Abbot advised Coleman to go to France, where there was a far more liberal attitude toward blacks and women pilots. She should work hard, save her money, and learn French.

While Coleman studied French, Abbott helped her find a flight school in France. He also gave her money for her trip and for living expenses. In doing so, he was not just being kind. He saw the potential importance for his newspaper in backing Coleman. If she succeeded in becoming the first African-American woman to earn a pilot's license, he and the *Chicago Defender* would reap the rewards of helping to "advance the race" in this way.

Coleman applied for her passport on November 4, 1920. On her application, she put January 20, 1896, as her birth date, pretending to be only 24, not 28. From then on, Bessie Coleman frequently lied about her age, but this practice was not unusual. At the time, a woman was supposed to be married by age twenty and was considered middle-aged at 40. Through no fault of her own, Bessie Coleman was getting a late start at her chosen career, and she didn't want her age to hinder her.

Just over two weeks later, Coleman began her adventure, sailing for England from New York City on the *S.S. Imparator*. From England, she crossed the English Channel to France on a boat-train and then made her way to Paris. In Paris, she began making applications to flight schools. The first refused to admit her because she was a woman; two women had lost their lives flying and the school did not wish to encourage a third to do so. The second school to which she applied accepted her, and turned out to be the most famous aviation school in France, the École d'Aviation des Frères Caudron (Aviation School of the Caudron Brothers) at the town of Le Crotoy in the region of France called the Somme.

Coleman learned to fly in a Nieuport Type 28, a French-made training airplane similar to the Curtiss JN-4D ("Jenny") that was used in the United States. It was twenty-seven feet in length with a forty-foot wing span. Made of wood, wire, aluminum, cloth, and pressed cardboard, it was lightweight but fragile. It had no steering wheel or brakes; the steering mechanism was a stick in front of the pilot and a rudder bar under the pilot's feet. Because it was a biplane, with room for two pilots, one behind the other, it was equipped with two sticks and two rudders; either, but not both, of which could be used to steer the plane. The braking system was a metal tail skid in the tail of the plane that, when the tail was lowered, dug into the earth after the plane reached the ground.

There was little protection from the elements, and Coleman soon understood why flyers dressed in leather flight jackets with helmets and scarves. The propellers made so much noise, and the wind sometimes howled so, that she could not hear the instructions of the teacher in the front seat and had to hold her steering mechanisms and feel what the

Bessie Coleman, nicknamed "Queen Bess, Daredevil Aviatrix."

teacher was doing with them. She was careful not to grasp them too tightly for fear of interfering with his actions. More than one student pilot had "frozen" at the controls and caused both flyers to die in a crash.

Coleman herself witnessed the death of a fellow student during her training, but it did not dissuade her from becoming a flyer.

After completing her seven-month course, Bessie Coleman took the test that qualified her for a license from the Fédération Aéronautique Internationale which at the time was the only organization that granted a flyer the right to fly anywhere in the world. She received her license on June 15, 1921, the first black woman ever to have done so.

When Coleman arrived back in New York in September 1921, she was greeted by both black and white reporters. The *Chicago Defender* had made certain to keep Americans abreast of Coleman's progress and accomplishments; and the return of the first American black woman licensed pilot was considered news even for white readers. Coleman used the press exposure to further enhance her reputation by telling reporters that she had ordered a Nieuport scout plane to be built for her in France.

Back in Chicago, Bessie Coleman gave a lengthy interview to a reporter for Robert Abbott's *Chicago*

Defender in which she explained her reason for wanting to fly: "We must have aviators if we are to keep up with the times. I shall never be satisfied until we have men of the Race who can fly. Do you know you have never lived until you have flown? Of course, it takes one with courage, nerve, and ambition. But I am thrilled to know we have men who are physically fit; now what is needed is men who are not afraid of death." She offered to teach anyone who wished to learn flying and stated that her dream was to start a flying school.

There is no question that Bessie Coleman had as her aim not just her own success but that of black people in general. She never denied her heritage for her own gain. Not long after she returned to Chicago, a reporter for the white *Chicago Herald* offered to do a story on her if she agreed to pass for white (with her copper-colored skin and features that looked Caucasian, she could have done so). She refused.

While she had achieved her goal of earning a pilot's license, Coleman knew she still had a long way to go if she wanted a career as a flyer or flight instructor. There were no commercial airlines at that time, and the war was over. The only thing for a flyer to do was to perform in air shows, also called air circuses because they featured stunts performed in the air. Coleman didn't have the training to do stunts.

She inquired around Chicago for someone to teach her, but again she found no one willing to do so. In February she returned to France for more training, and while in Europe also visited Holland and Germany. On her arrival back in the United States, she glibly told reporters that she had ordered a dozen Dutch-made Fokker airplanes for her aviation school.

On Labor Day, September 3, 1922, Bessie Coleman appeared in her first air show in New York City. The event was in honor of the Fifteenth New York Infantry, part of the all-black 369th American Expeditionary Force that had served in World War I. Considering the buildup given her appearance by the *Chicago Defender*, the several thousand in attendance expected to see some stunt flying, but Coleman was not allowed to perform any stunts. Not having an airplane of her own, although she was in the habit of telling reporters that she was expecting special orders of them, she had to borrow one. The Curtiss JN-4D arrived with a company pilot who went along with her on her first takeoff, just to make sure she knew what she was doing. Satisfied, he allowed her to fly alone the next time. But the company forbade her to do any stunts in

Bessie Coleman in her plane, the Curtiss JN-4D or "Jenny."

its plane. The assembled crowd had to be content with having witnessed the "first public flight of a black woman in this country," as one newspaper reporter put it.

Coleman might have been considerably upstaged by the appearance at the same event of Hubert F. Julian. But while Julian's stunts certainly were more exciting than Coleman's rather conservative flights, the mere fact that she was a black *woman* flyer made her the star of the show.

While in New York, Coleman signed a contract to star in a film to be financed by the African-American Seminole Film Producing Company, tentatively titled *Shadow and Sunshine*. In the full-length feature film, she was to play a black woman flyer. J. A. Jackson, a black critic for *Billboard* magazine who had given Coleman's flying rave reviews, had an interest in the film company and was the one who signed her to the contract. It seemed a perfect way for Coleman to publicize herself and her flying ability.

By the time Coleman returned to Chicago late in September 1922, she was a celebrity. "Queen Bess, Daredevil Aviatrix," as she was dubbed by reporters, made her Chicago debut in an air show at the Checkerboard Airdrome the following month. In this show, she flew a plane owned by David Behncke, a white businessman who owned the aerodrome and sponsored many air shows there. He saw no reason not to let a black woman flyer borrow one of his planes. For Bessie Coleman, performing for crowds in her adopted hometown was a great thrill.

Not long after her Chicago debut, Coleman returned to New York City at the African-American

Seminole Film Producing Company's expense to start filming *Shadow and Sunshine*. But when she learned that in her first scene she was to wear raggedy clothing, carry her belongings on her back and use a walking stick, and portray an ignorant girl arriving in New York, she backed out. Her pride in her race would not allow her to portray such a demeaning stereotype.

J. A. Jackson was furious. Using his power as a reporter, he began to spread the word that she was unreliable. And his power was considerable, for he was not only on the *Billboard* payroll but also on the East Coast staff of the Associated Negro Press, a Chicago-based wire service used by most of the African-American weekly newspapers in the country. Alienating him was a big mistake for Coleman's career; and yet, she felt she could not have done otherwise, for she felt the dignity of blacks had been at stake in the conflict over the film role.

Publicly, Coleman continued to assure reporters that the only thing standing between her and her planned flight school was the arrival of planes she had ordered specially built. As if to give her dream a semblance of reality, she opened a small office in Chicago and persuaded David Behncke, owner of Checkerboard Airdrome, to lend her a plane in which to give instruction.

One of her students was Robert Paul Sachs, an African American who was the midwestern advertising manager for the Coast Tire and Rubber Company, based in Oakland, California. On learning what her student's business was, Coleman offered to do some air advertising, dropping advertisements from an airplane. The fee she proposed would help finance the purchase of an airplane. Coast Tire and Rubber agreed, and in late January Coleman boarded a train out of Chicago bound for California and a new start.

California was already a center for the new flying craze. Its moderate climate was good for the fragile aircraft. Its growing importance as a center for the motion picture industry also helped flyers, for in their own way they were entertainment stars, too. Already, aviator Amelia Earhart was staging exhibition flights in a plane built by Bert Kinner and was endorsing his planes. French actress André Peyre frequently appeared with Earhart, hoping to gain publicity for her acting career with her exhibition flights.

On arriving in California, Coleman went first to Oakland for a tour of the Coast Tire and Rubber Company. By the time she left Oakland for Los Angeles, she had the money to buy her own plane, so she must have persuaded company officials of the value of her publicity potential. In Los Angeles, she went to the Rockwell Army Intermediate Depot, where the military kept surplus planes. For $400, Bessie got an old Curtiss JN-4D, the early, popular training plane. It was still in its crate and required assembling.

While she waited for her plane to be ready, Coleman started looking for financial backers for an exhibition. Before long, she had arranged to be part of the celebration of the opening of a new fairgrounds at Palomar Park in Los Angeles.

Coleman was happy and excited on the morning of February 11, 1923, as she made her way to the Santa Monica airfield for the short, 25-mile flight to the fairgrounds. At last, her dream seemed to be coming true. She had her own plane and a chance to show what she could do in it. She was certain that her exhibition show would get wide publicity, and she intended to use that publicity to attract backers for her flight school.

Wearing her full flight regalia, Coleman climbed into her own "Jenny" and made ready for takeoff. An airfield worker started the propeller moving; Coleman adjusted her helmet and set to work at the controls. The plane lifted off the ground easily. Then, 300 feet in the air, the engine stalled, and the plane went into a nosedive. By the time it crashed

A formal portrait of Bessie Coleman in her flying gear.

onto the airstrip, Coleman was unconscious and seriously injured. She suffered a broken leg, fractured ribs, many cuts on her face, and internal injuries.

When she regained consciousness, all Coleman could think of was the air show. She begged the doctor who examined her to "patch her up" so she could go on to Palomar. Instead, the doctor called an ambulance and sent her to the hospital.

On hearing that there would be no air show starring Bessie Coleman, the predominantly black crowd booed and hissed. Instead of being worried about the condition of the first black female pilot, they worried that they had paid money for a show that wasn't going to take place. Their reaction must have hurt Coleman, but publicly she said nothing about it. Instead, from her hospital bed, she sent a message to those who wished her well: "Tell them all that as soon as I can walk I'm going to fly!"

While still in the hospital waiting for her leg to heal, she placed an advertisement in the African-American newspaper, the *California Eagle*, for the Coleman School of Aeronautics. Tuition was $400 ($25 on signing a contract and the rest payable in installments). The students were to be responsible for any injuries they sustained; and Coleman was to be the judge of whether or not they were competent to fly an airplane.

Coleman had little money herself, but she did have the continued support of her former student in Chicago, the businessman Robert Sachs. He took up a collection at his company's office and urged the black people of California to help pay Coleman's hospital bills, which must have been considerable. She did not leave the hospital until early May, nearly three months after her accident, and even then her leg remained in a cast.

In June, Coleman returned to Chicago to start over. By the end of the month, she had scheduled an exhibition for Labor Day at Driving Park in Columbus, Ohio. But she was disappointed in the lack of interest on the part of the *Chicago Defender*. The newspaper had run a brief mention about her return to the city, but did not help publicize her upcoming air show. Instead, the *Evening Dispatch*, a white paper published in Columbus, provided her with the necessary publicity. The paper described her as "the only colored aviatrix in the world" and stated that she was 23 years old (she was actually 31). But it rained on Labor Day, and once again Coleman was denied the opportunity to show what she could do.

Coleman returned to Columbus one week after Labor Day for the exhibition that had been rained out a week earlier. This time there were no mishaps, and she performed for crowds estimated to number 10,000. She then announced that she was going on a tour of the South, but the tour never happened. There were rumors of trouble with her latest manager.

Whatever had occurred, Coleman's career was on hold for a year and a half until she finally found interest in her story in Texas and lined up a series of lectures and exhibition flights.

Coleman arrived in Houston, Texas, in May 1925, and immediately began to give lectures and to excite considerable interest on the part of the press. She told reporters that she was 23 years old (she was now 33) and that her greatest ambition was to "uplift the colored race" by establishing a flying school.

June 19, 1925, was the date of her first flight in Texas. A local black flyer named Captain R. W. Mackie was in charge of the show in Houston, and it was he who probably provided Coleman with the JN-4D that she piloted in the show. So great was the pre-show publicity that both whites and blacks wished to attend, and the show's operators had to arrange for a special section for whites at a show that had been planned for an exclusively black audience.

Coleman took off in the plane and ascended high into the air, then deliberately stalled the plane's motor and dove to within a few feet of the ground before pulling up and away. It was a sequence so similar to the near-fatal flight in which she had crashed that it was probably not just the crowd who let out a roar of relief but Coleman herself. She then executed a series of dives, barrel rolls, figure eights, and loop-the-loops to the great exultation of the audience.

Spectators at the event could, for a fee, take rides in airplanes at the old speedway auto racetrack that had been renamed Houston Aerial Transport Field in honor of the event. It was thus an historic occasion for another reason, for it marked the first time blacks in the South were able to go up in an airplane. That day, approximately 75 black people took the opportunity. Most of them were women, perhaps a testimonial to Bessie Coleman's influence.

Coleman's remarks to the press began to focus more on black women. The press seemed to appreciate her achievements more than those of black men. Coleman also understood that the majority of white society was more likely to accept black females in new roles than black males, who were considered more threatening.

For her next air show, in San Antonio, Coleman persuaded a black San Antonio woman, Liza Dilworth, to make a parachute jump from the wing of Coleman's plane at 1,000 feet. Dilworth was frightened, and justifiably so, given the recent deaths of flyers in Texas air circuses. Fortunately, nothing happened to Coleman's plane, and Dilworth made a successful jump, to the excitement of the assembled crowd.

As the months wore on, Coleman gave more lectures and fewer exhibitions, for she believed that she could actually interest more African Americans in flying by telling of her experiences and showing film clips of her career. Also, giving lectures was

A billboard to promote a black air circus, similar to the ones Bessie Coleman performed in.

far less expensive and complicated than arranging air circuses. But with the money she earned from the lectures, she planned to buy another airplane, for her dream was still to start her own flight school.

When she had the money in hand, Coleman went to Love Field in Dallas, where there was a great variety of used aircraft available for purchase. She chose a plane, probably another JN-4D, but this one with the slightly advanced OX-5 engine. Unfortunately, it cost more money than she had.

On September 5 and 6, Coleman was scheduled to give two shows in Wharton, southwest of Houston. She had advertised a parachute jump by Liza Dilworth, but on the first day Dilworth backed out. Not wanting to disappoint her audiences, Coleman decided that she herself would not only fly but also make the jump the next day. She wired to Houston for a pilot to fly her plane so she could make the jump; and at the air show she both piloted and jumped before a delighted audience.

Coleman next gave a show in Waxahachie, where she had grown up. The audience was to be mixed, and the original plan was for separate entrances to the show as well as separate seating areas. Coleman balked at the idea of separate entrances and prevailed; but seating would be separate as originally planned. It was one of the most satisfying shows

Bessie Coleman gave, for many in the audience were hometown folk who had known her as a girl.

Coleman gave several other shows in Texas. Altogether, it was the most sustained successful period of her career, for there were no mishaps, accidents, or cancellations because of weather. The press coverage she received was consistently good, and she came to believe again that her goal of having her own school was in reach.

Coleman returned to Chicago, then on Christmas Day, 1925, set out on a lecture tour of the South. In Orlando, Florida, she was taken under the wing of a prominent black couple, the Hills. The Reverend Hezakiah Hill was pastor of Mount Zion Missionary Baptist Institutional Church, and his wife was a community activist. Both believed that Coleman's desire to "uplift the race" deserved the greatest hearing in Orlando, and they invited her to stay with them. Coleman gratefully accepted the offer, and soon she had come to regard the Hills as surrogate parents. She called them Mother and Daddy, joined their church, and became very religious.

Under the particular influence of Mrs. Hill, who disapproved of Coleman's raising money for her flight school by doing stunt flying and parachute jumps, Coleman opened a beauty salon in Orlando.

But she accepted an invitation to do a parachute

jump at the Orlando Chamber of Commerce's annual flower show before she learned that it was for whites only. On learning that African Americans would not be allowed in, Coleman refused to do the stunt unless they were admitted. Remarkably for the time (Orlando was highly segregated), the chamber of commerce backed down and blacks were allowed to attend. Coleman did the jump as promised.

Whether it was as a result of the flower show or some other event, Coleman soon met the benefactor she'd been hoping to meet for years. Edwin M. Beeman was young, married, white, and the heir to a family chewing-gum fortune. Although there was gossip about him and Coleman, it is likely that his interest in her mainly reflected his interest in flying and flying machines. Beeman gave Coleman the remaining money she needed to get her plane from Dallas, Texas, and have it flown to Jacksonville, Florida, where she was scheduled to do an exhibition on May 1. Coleman was elated.

On April 27, before she departed from Orlando to take a train to Jacksonville and await the arrival of her plane, Coleman promised the Hills that she would make Orlando her home base and would stop doing exhibitions in favor of lecturing and teaching.

Meanwhile, 24-year-old William D. Wills, who

was white, set off from Dallas's Love Field for Jacksonville in Coleman's JN-4D, encountering considerable difficulty along the way. The old OX-5 engine, which was supposed to be capable of doing 90 miles an hour, barely made 60 mph. It malfunctioned twice, forcing the pilot to make two unscheduled landings in Mississippi in addition to the three planned landings. What he said to Coleman about the plane and its engine after he arrived in Jacksonville on April 28 is not known.

Early the next morning, John Betsch of the Jacksonville Negro Welfare League that was the sponsor of the show, picked up Coleman and then Wills and drove them to Jacksonville's Paxon Field, where Coleman's "Jenny" was parked. At the field, Wills examined the plane and declared it ready. Coleman then knelt beside it and prayed—something she had taken to doing since moving in with the Hills in Orlando. She then climbed into the rear of the plane, asking Wills to take over the controls in the cockpit so she could study the field for a good jump site. She did not buckle her seatbelt because it would have prevented her from leaning over to study the ground.

Wills took the plane up and headed for the racetrack. Once over the racetrack, he circled for some five minutes at 2,000 feet, then climbed to 3,500 feet and turned back for Paxon Field. He was cruising at about 80 mph when suddenly the plane accelerated to 110 mph and went into a nosedive. At about 1,000 feet it went into a tailspin, and then flipped over at 500 feet.

Unprotected by a seatbelt, Coleman tumbled out. Her body flipped end over end through the air before falling with a thud to the ground. She died on impact, nearly every bone in her body broken.

Meanwhile, Wills tried to regain control of the plane, but without success. The plane crashed into farmland about 1,000 feet from where Coleman's body lay. Betsch had rushed to the site, and was so upset that, without thinking, he lit a cigarette. The match ignited gasoline fumes from the plane, and the aircraft immediately went up in flames. Wills died in the conflagration. Betsch was arrested and taken to Jacksonville jail, but no charges were brought against him.

Investigators later discovered the cause of the accident; a wrench left on the floor of the plane had slid into the gears and jammed them. A newer plane would have had protective covering for its gears.

Coleman's body was moved to an African-American funeral home. Wills's body was transported to a white hospital to await his brother, who would take the remains back to Texas for burial.

Coleman's first funeral was held the following day and was attended by more than 5,000 people. After the funeral, her body was placed aboard a train bound for Orlando, where the Hills had arranged another service so that her many friends in Orlando could mourn her as well.

After that service, Viola Hill accompanied Coleman's body on the last leg of its journey. As the train pulled into Chicago's Forty-third Street Station, several thousand people were waiting, as was a military escort from the African-American Eighth Infantry Regiment of the Illinois National Guard, which took the body to the funeral home on the South Side of the city. There, her body lay in its coffin as an estimated 10,000 people filed by to pay their last respects.

The next morning, Coleman's body was taken to Pilgrim Baptist Church for her final funeral, which was attended by thousands more. The Reverend Junius C. Austin, pastor of the church, referred in his eulogy to the irony of so much support for Bessie Coleman in death: "This girl was one hundred years ahead of the Race she loved so well, and by whom she was least appreciated."

Bessie Coleman inspired many other African Americans in aviation. But as the years passed, the memory of her dimmed and few Americans, black or white, were aware that there had been an African-American woman flyer so early in aviation history.

3

THE 1930s

I T was logical for northern urban centers that attracted large black populations to also become
centers for black aviation. But this was not true of
New York City, whose Harlem represented the largest concentration of African Americans in the nation, if not the world. Although Hubert Julian first
made his mark in aviation as the Black Eagle in
Harlem, he had to go elsewhere to make a living at
flying.

Two cities that were especially important in the
growth and development of black aviation were Los
Angeles and Chicago. Los Angeles became a center
for the aviation industry in general because of its
importance in aircraft manufacturing and its large
stockpile of World War I surplus airplanes. After
the war, although production of military airplanes
decreased, and many former workers in the aviation
industry were out of work, Los Angeles contained

the largest aircraft stockpiles. These surplus airplanes were available for purchase by anyone with the money.

Just as white flyers were attracted to Los Angeles, so were black flyers, among them William J. Powell, a businessman and native of Chicago, who in 1929 founded the Bessie Coleman Aero Club in that city in honor of the woman pilot who had died in a tragic accident four years earlier. Powell supported many young black flyers in the days when mentors were few and far between.

Born in Henderson, Kentucky, in 1897, Powell, as a youngster, moved to Chicago with his family. The family was middle class, and Powell was a good student. On graduating from Wendell Phillips High School, he entered the engineering program at the University of Illinois at Champaign.

In 1917, when the United States entered World War I, Powell's college education made it possible for him to be one of the few African Americans to enlist in the segregated armed services with the goal of becoming an officer. He attended army officer training school in Chillicothe, Ohio, although he and the other black trainees were segregated from the white officers-to-be. When he left the training school, he was awarded the rank of lieutenant and shipped out to fight in Europe. He had

William J. Powell, a business man, sponsored many young black flyers.

almost completed his tour of duty when his all-black unit was sent to the front lines. With his unit under heavy attack, Powell suffered a severe barrage of poison gas and had to be evacuated from the field of battle. The gassing ended his military career, and he was sent back to the United States to recuperate.

Although Powell would never fully recover from the gassing, his health was restored enough for him to open a service station in Chicago. He quickly built up the business until he eventually had four stations and a large garage. He kept up his ties to the military and was a member of the American Legion, attending monthly meetings and annual conventions. At one such convention in Paris, France, in 1925, Powell took his first ride in an airplane. His life was changed forever by that exhilarating experience, and he returned to Chicago determined to become a flyer.

Like Bessie Coleman before him, Powell could not find a flight school in the Chicago area that would accept him. But he would not give up on his idea of flying and succeeded in gaining admittance to a school in Los Angeles. Having done well in business, he could pay the $1,000 tuition for a few months' training.

There was another reason why Los Angeles appealed to him. Its dry, mild climate was better for his health than the humidity and cold of Chicago. Against the wishes of his family, he sold his garage and service stations and relocated in Los Angeles.

Powell's obsession with flying was more than just personal. His military experience caused him to envision major breakthroughs in the way wars were fought. His engineering background helped him understand that aviation was a new technology that could revolutionize twentieth-century life. It would change not only how people traveled but how goods were moved from one place to another. He firmly believed that if African Americans could get into aviation in the early stages, their achievements would help their condition in America generally. He envisioned blacks in all areas of the aviation industry, not just as pilots but also as designers and engineers and flight-school operators.

To spread his message, in the same year he moved to Los Angeles to attend flight school Powell persuaded two like-minded black businessmen to form a black aviation club, which they envisioned as just the first of more than 100 clubs throughout the nation. They named the club after Bessie Coleman, for she, too, had been convinced that aviation was an important path toward social equality for blacks.

The Bessie Coleman Aero Club functioned not just as a society for African-American flyers but also operated the Bessie Coleman School, realizing the dream that Coleman herself was never able to. At that time no special license was needed to operate a flight school. Additionally, the club maintained a workshop where members could both build their own planes and repair war-surplus planes.

The stock market crash of 1929 and the resulting onset of the Great Depression did nothing to dampen the spirits of the businessman and vision-

William J. Powell at the Bessie Coleman Aero Club which he founded in 1929 in honor of Bessie Coleman's dream.

ary, William J. Powell. He was convinced that flying was not a hobby or a luxury but an infant industry that would grow no matter what happened to the nation's economy. He was more eager than ever to spread the word about blacks in aviation, and to this end the Bessie Coleman Aero Club sponsored the first all-black air show in Los Angeles on Labor Day, 1931. The event attracted a crowd estimated at 15,000 and so impressed officials of the city that they asked the club to organize a second air show to raise money for the city's unemployment fund, which was shrinking alarmingly as the Depression grew worse.

Among the first students at the Bessie Coleman Aero Club flight school was a young woman named Marie Coker. She was part of that second all-black air show on December 6, 1931. The featured performer was Hubert Fauntleroy Julian. Coker later recalled, "There were only five [black] people flying out here in California, and when Julian came out that made six. So there were Five Blackbirds and one parachute jumper. . . . I would be the last one to go up. And everybody came to see this girl fly. I did my figure eights. I did my spiral. . . . We were called the Five Blackbirds because that is the first time in history that five black people were in the air at one time."

William Powell had a vision, and he tried many ways to instill his vision in others, especially young blacks. In 1934 he self-published his autobiography, entitled *Black Wings*. Dedicated to Bessie Coleman, it urged young blacks "to fill the air with black wings." The publicity flyer for the book was headlined: "One Million Jobs for Negroes," and went on to proclaim:

READ BLACK WINGS
Are Negroes planning to quit riding the
segregated railroads and busses in the South?
READ BLACK WINGS
Why are so few Negroes in Business and
Industry?
EVERY AMERICAN SHOULD READ
THIS BOOK
Send money order for $2.00 and book will
be mailed to you—Postage Prepaid.

For a short time in the middle 1930s, Powell also published a magazine, *Craftsmen Aero News*, which he hoped would appeal to other black flyers and aircraft builders. But the magazine didn't attract a substantial readership and publication soon ceased.

William J. Powell, however, was successful in at-

FIRST TRANS-CONTINENTAL FLIGHT
Los Angeles to New York
October 9th 1932. Flying Time 41 hrs 27 min.

J. Herman Banning and Thomas C. Allen were the first African Americans to fly cross-country.

tracting young black people to flying. His most successful protégé was James Herman Banning.

Banning was born in 1900 in Canton, Oklahoma, which at that time was not a state but was known as "Indian territory." Many blacks had moved to the area after the Civil War seeking relief from the segregation of the South and also searching for the greater opportunities that the American frontier seemed to offer.

Young Banning showed special skill at mathematics and working with machines; he was very young when he started repairing the family's farm machines and automobiles. He discovered airplanes when he was in high school. In 1914 World War I had begun in Europe, and Banning was fascinated by newsreel footage of fighter craft doing battle in the skies. He made a point of learning all he could about aircraft and flying.

On graduation from high school, Banning worked for a year to save money for college. In 1919, after he was accepted at Iowa State College, which had an excellent engineering program, his parents rented their farm in Oklahoma and moved to Ames, Iowa, with him.

In Ames, Banning opened a repair shop in his parents' garage to make extra money while he pursued his engineering studies at Iowa State, where he was one of only a few black students. He continued his hobby of reading and learning everything he could about airplanes, and in 1920 he got his first opportunity to ride in one. He paid five dollars at an air circus to take a ride in a Canuck biplane piloted by World War I combat pilot, Stanley Doyle. From that time on, he dreamed of becoming a pilot.

Banning's auto repair business did so well that

after two years he dropped out of Iowa State and devoted himself full-time to the business. He continued to dream of flying, but although his area of Iowa was a very active aviation center he could not find a flight school that would accept him. Nor was he successful in gaining admittance to a flight school in Chicago. In 1924, in Des Moines, Iowa, he finally found another World War I ace, Lieutenant Raymond C. Fisher, to teach him; and once he knew how to fly, he used his profits from the auto repair business to buy his own Hummingbird biplane, naming it *Miss Ames*. In 1926, when the United States Department of Commerce introduced the nation's first aviation licensing laws, Banning became the first African-American pilot to be licensed in America.

Over the next three years, Banning devoted all his time to flying. He barnstormed all over the country, but kept in mind the potentials for business in aviation by also flying mail and other cargo. Out in Los Angeles, William J. Powell learned of Banning and excitedly realized that he was just the sort of young man to be chief pilot at the Bessie Coleman Aero Club. Powell also encouraged Banning in his dream of making a cross-country flight.

Banning could not afford to buy a new plane, so he purchased a war-surplus craft called an Eagle

Rock. Its engine was fourteen years old, so Banning knew he would have to have a skilled mechanic to take care of it. He found one in Thomas C. Allen. The two then attempted to raise the necessary money for their trip.

They quickly ran into the racial barriers that plagued African Americans in every venture: White businesses were unwilling to stake them, for a black cross-country flight would do nothing for their businesses. Undeterred, Banning and Allen dubbed themselves the "Flying Hobos" and decided to make it across the country by seeking contributions from black communities along the way. With barely $100, they took off from Los Angeles on September 18, 1932, bent on reaching New York.

One hundred dollars was hardly enough to pay for the gasoline and oil they needed to fly cross-country, not to mention food and lodging. But Banning and Allen believed they could count on the help of other African Americans, and they were right. Whenever they had to land to refuel or were forced down by bad weather, they sought the black sections of town, where they were fed and lodged without cost and sometimes given donations of money taken up in collections. As Banning and Allen slowly made their way east, their impossible dream attracted national attention as everyone wondered whether or not they would make it.

The white press picked up on the story, and whites stepped forward or, when approached by Banning and Allen, agreed to help them. A businessman in Tulsa, Oklahoma, named William Skelly, arranged for them to buy gas and oil on credit. White students in St. Louis, Missouri, helped them find the source of the engine trouble when they were forced to land at that city. In Pittsburgh, Pennsylvania, a worker for the Franklin Delano Roosevelt Democratic presidential campaign arranged for them to drop thousands of campaign fliers between Pennsylvania and New York in return for the money needed to fly back to Los Angeles.

The old Eagle Rock landed in Valley Stream, Long Island, on October 9, 1932, and Banning and Allen had become the first African Americans to fly cross-country. Although it had taken them three weeks to do it, their actual time in the air had been less than two days.

New York City gave the two men a hero's welcome, including the keys to the city by Mayor Jimmy Walker. On their return to Los Angeles, they were also celebrated for their feat.

Sadly, just four months later, Banning was killed at an air show in San Diego, California, when a biplane in which he was a passenger crashed to the ground. Only 32 years old when he died, Banning's death was a great loss to black aviation.

In 1933, the year following James Herbert Banning's transcontinental flight, Atlantic City, New Jersey, became part of the history of black aviation when C. Alfred Anderson and Dr. Albert E. Forsythe became the first black aviators to successfully complete

C. Alfred Anderson and Dr. Albert E. Forsythe arriving in Los Angeles after completing the first leg of their round-trip transcontinental flight.

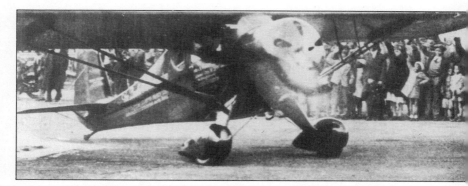

C. Alfred Anderson and Albert E. Forsythe (in plane) at the send-off for their Pan-American Goodwill Flight in 1933.

a round-trip transcontinental flight from Atlantic City, New Jersey, to Los Angeles, California, and back. The two black natives of Philadelphia called their Fairchild 24 plane *Pride of Atlantic City* for the occasion. As in the case of James Herbert Banning, they made several stops to rest and refuel each way, although they did not have the same money problems as Banning. In fact, Anderson and Forsythe made sure their trip was well planned and well financed before they ever set out.

Having attracted considerable publicity, and much goodwill, as a result of their 1933 transcontinental round-trip, the following year the two planned an even more daring endeavor: a long-distance flight they called the Pan-American or Goodwill Flight. For this flight they chose a Lambert

Monocoupe, which they named the *Spirit of Booker T. Washington* in honor of the noted black educator who had founded Tuskegee Institute, the premier African-American college in Alabama. Robert R. Moton, President of Tuskegee Institute, and his wife attended the christening ceremonies.

The first leg of their journey was a flight from Miami, Florida, to Nassau, the Bahamas, the first time such a flight had been made in a land plane rather than a seaplane. Nassau did not have an airport, nor even an airstrip, so Anderson and Forsythe had to land on a dirt road. They did so at night, with only the headlights of automobiles to see by, showing remarkable skill. The governor of the Bahamas greeted the two Americans; American diplomats there, as well as elsewhere along the journey, were also supportive of the Goodwill Flight. The population of the Caribbean was largely black, and the flight of two African Americans was recognized by the U.S. State Department as reflecting well on opportunities for blacks in the United States.

Anderson and Forsythe then proceeded to make stops in Havana, Cuba; Jamaica; Haiti; the Dominican Republic; Puerto Rico; the Virgin Islands; Grenada; Trinidad; and Guyana (formerly British Guyana). Unfortunately, on their return flight from an improvised airstrip in Trinidad, the two pilots damaged the *Spirit of Booker T. Washington* and were unable to complete the return journey. Nevertheless, their Goodwill Flight had been a huge success, attracting worldwide attention and giving black Americans reason to be very proud.

Perhaps the most important center of black aviation in the 1930s was Chicago, where Bessie Coleman had gotten her start. Indeed, it might be said that Chicago became an important center for black aviation in part *because* of the pioneering efforts of Bessie Coleman.

Not long after her death, a group of blacks in the city were determined to honor Bessie Coleman's legacy. One year after her death, a memorial stone was unveiled at her grave, paid for with donations from friends and well-wishers. In 1931, a group of black pilots from the Chicago area flew over her grave and dropped flowers on it. But from the first, they knew they could honor her memory best by promoting black aviation.

With the help of the local chapter of the National Association for the Advancement of Colored People (NAACP), these black pilots pressured Curtiss-Wright, a large airplane manufacturing company headquartered in Chicago, to admit African

Willa Brown (left) and Janet Waterford Bragg (right) were the only female members of the first all-black class at Curtiss-Wright Aeronautical School.

Americans to its flight training school. The company relented, and established an all-black class in 1930. The company would not even consider integrating its classes, fearing—no doubt correctly—that its white students would object. That first all-black class consisted of nine students, and included two women, Willa Brown and Janet Waterford Bragg. In addition to flight training, the students

Cornelius R. Coffey (right foreground) was part of the first all-black class at the Curtiss-Wright Aeronautical School.

received instruction in airplane mechanics, for in those days any serious pilot also wanted to know how his or her plane worked and how to fix the many things that could go wrong.

Cornelius R. Coffey was in that first class. Like

James Herbert Banning, he was an automobile mechanic by trade. He later established his own flight training school, the Coffey School of Aeronautics, and founded the National Airmen's Association.

John C. Robinson was another member of that first all-black class at Curtiss-Wright. Robinson also organized the first black flying club in Chicago, the Challenger Air Pilots' Association. Since local white airports excluded black flyers at that time, the club built its own airstrip in the all-black township of Robbins, Illinois, near Chicago, in 1933. Unfortunately, a sudden windstorm destroyed the hangar at the Robbins Airport not long after it opened. The Challenger Air Pilots' Association then moved its operations to Harlem Airport near Chicago; and Robinson secured the club's first airplane by trading his automobile in exchange for a Hummingbird. (According to some sources, Janet Waterford Bragg, the registered nurse who was in the first class at Curtiss-Wright flight training school, was responsible for buying the first aircraft for the Challenger Air Pilots' Association.) Robinson joined Hubert Julian in Ethiopia to attempt to build that country's first national air force. But after Benito Mussolini ordered the invasion of Ethiopia, Robinson returned to the United States and concentrated on building black aeronautics closer to home.

While the founders of the Challenger Air Pilots' Association would be justifiably proud of their efforts, they realized that their organization was too small to make a significant impact in the field of African-American aviation. Only a major institution could do that. The largest black educational institution in the country was Tuskegee Institute. It had strong programs in engineering and mechanics, and several members of the association flew to Tuskegee to urge the school's administration to start an aviation program. The conservative-thinking administration did not share the view of the Chicago flyers that aviation was the wave of the future, and the flyers realized they had made the trip for nothing. On top of that disappointment, the trip proved to be extremely hazardous and the club's airplane was damaged.

Next, members of the Challenger Air Pilots' Association approached the United States government. Congress had authorized the establishment of the Civilian Pilot Training program (CPT) in 1938 to train private citizens as pilots so that in the event of war there would be a pool of trained flyers to pilot the nation's airplanes. The group was more successful this time. Major organizations, such as the NAACP, also pressured the CPT to admit blacks. In 1939, Cornelius Coffey's National Airmen's

Association, and the *Chicago Defender*, sponsored a round-trip flight from Chicago to Washington, DC, to dramatize the importance of opening aviation to African Americans. The pilots who flew that exhibition were Chicagoans Dale L. White and

Dr. A. Porter Davis (left), Willa Brown (center), and Cornelius R. Coffey (right) at a National Airman's Association meet at Chicago's Harlem Airport, 1939.

71

Chauncey E. Spencer. Arriving in Washington, DC, they and Cornelius Coffey met with Missouri Senator Harry S. Truman and other dignitaries and pressed for more government support of black aviation. That same year, the government opened the CPT program to African-American applicants.

With this change in government policy, Tuskegee Institute finally became involved in black aviation and established a Division of Aeronautics to train black pilots under the CPT program. C. Alfred Anderson, of the Anderson-Forsythe long-distance flights, was hired as chief primary flight instructor. Other schools that participated in CPT included Hampton Institute in Virginia; Howard University in Washington, DC; and the Coffey School of Aeronautics in Chicago, which also cooperated with Wendell Phillips High School to offer classes in aviation mechanics. A large number of black pilots were trained in the CPT program; but in some ways it proved to be a mixed blessing. Once trained, they found there were hardly any opportunities to use their piloting skills. They were not content to do stunts in air shows. They wanted to be part of the growing commercial uses of aviation and to employ their skills to serve their country in war, should the United States enter the expanding conflict in Europe.

Thus, as the 1940s began, there were more opportunities for black flyers, but far fewer than there were for whites. The novelist Richard Wright alluded to the barriers that stood in the way of a young black child in a conversation between two black youths in Chicago in his 1940 novel *Native Son:* The two watch an airplane performing intricate maneuvers in the air above them, and one boy announces that he could fly a plane if he had the chance. The other boy scoffs, "If you wasn't black and if you had some money and if they'd let you go to that aviation school, you could fly a plane."

4

WORLD WAR II—
THE TRIUMPHS

WAR had raged in Europe for two years, and the United States had not entered the conflict directly. But after Japan bombed the United States naval base at Pearl Harbor in Hawaii on December 7, 1941, the United States entered the war on both the European and Pacific fronts.

Even before its official entry into the war, the United States had geared up for conflict. Aviation had taken on great importance in the war in Europe. Japanese bombers would soon destroy the U.S. fleet at Pearl Harbor. The United States manufacture of war planes had been made an immediate national priority, as was the training of pilots to fly them. The Civilian Pilots Training program was renamed the War Training Service program (WTS), and the U.S. Army Air Corps, the Army's aviation division, looked to graduates of the program for its personnel.

As great as the Army's need for trained pilots was, the service had no plans to include blacks in its Air Corps. The administration of President Franklin Delano Roosevelt, however, had other ideas. Responding to pressure to include blacks in the nation's war mobilization plans, in 1940, before the November presidential election, Roosevelt issued a directive to the War Department to create a black flying unit. The War Department looked at the armed services and decided that the all-white Army Air Corps was a likely target for change. The Army established a base at Tuskegee Institute, Tuskegee Army Airfield. The training program inaugurated there became known as the "Tuskegee Experiment" because, as Lieutenant General Benjamin O. Davis, Jr., put it in his 1991 autobiography, "In 1941 the Army still regarded all blacks as totally inferior to whites—somewhat less than human, and certainly incapable of contributing positively to its combat mission."

The Chief of the Army Air Corps chose Davis, a career army man like his father before him, to head the new unit and ordered him released from his duties at Fort Riley in Kansas to begin pilot training.

The story of Benjamin O. Davis, Jr., is the story of blacks in the military, and especially in military aviation, from the early 1940s to the 1960s. Davis

Brigadier General Benjamin O. Davis (left), who, in 1942, was the only black general in the U.S. Army.

personally lived through the rabid segregation of the prewar and early war years, the softening of attitudes on the part of the military hierarchy, and finally, the full integration of the U.S. flying service.

Benjamin O. Davis, Jr., was born in Washington, DC, on December 18, 1912. At that time, his father was a first lieutenant of cavalry at Fort Russell in

Wyoming. Benjamin O. Davis, Sr., had experienced much racial discrimination in the Army, but he had not let that stop him from pursuing a career he loved. He was so exceptional that he managed to earn a Regular Army commission in a time when that was practically unheard of for a black man. In gaining a Regular Army commission as a second lieutenant of cavalry in 1901, Benjamin O. Davis, Sr., joined the only other black regular officer in the Army, Charles Young, who had graduated from Army officers training school at West Point in 1889.

But the Army was concerned about assigning a black officer to a situation in which he would command white enlisted men or outrank white officers. So, the senior Davis always received "safe" assignments, such as teaching military tactics or commanding Reserve Officers Training Corps (ROTC) at black colleges, commanding black National Guard units, or serving as a military attaché abroad.

In 1916, Benjamin, Jr.'s, mother died after giving birth to her third child. Their father cared for the children with the help of two of his late wife's sisters until he was assigned to duty in the Philippines. The three Davis children went to live with their paternal grandparents in Washington, DC, when Benjamin was five.

After three years in the Philippines, during which

he courted by mail and then married a family friend, the elder Benjamin Davis was assigned to the position of professor of military science and tactics at Tuskegee Institute. As soon as the couple had settled in, the three children joined their father and new stepmother and began life as a family in the all-black town of Tuskegee, Alabama.

Four years later, they moved to Cleveland, Ohio, where the elder Davis had been assigned to the position of instructor for a black National Guard unit. In the summer of 1926, while his parents were in Europe, Benjamin, Jr., stayed with his relatives in Washington, DC. While there, he saw his first air show. His uncle Ernest took him one Sunday afternoon to watch the barnstormers at Bolling Field, which at that time was a simple, dirt strip. Young Benjamin enjoyed watching the acrobatics so much that when his parents returned from Europe he persuaded his father to take him to Bolling Field again. His father even paid the five dollars the barnstormer charged to take young Benjamin for his first airplane ride. Five dollars was no small sum in those days.

Benjamin, Jr., was so thrilled by the experience that he determined to be a pilot. The following year, Charles Lindbergh made his famous transatlantic flight, and Benjamin read all the news accounts he could find about the feat. It seemed to him the most exciting thing in the world to be a pilot.

Davis attended an integrated high school in Cleveland, served as student council president, and graduated at the top of his class when he was only sixteen years old. The summer after graduation, he took summer school classes at Fisk University in Nashville, Tennessee, because his stepmother wanted him to experience life at a black college. That fall, he entered Case Western Reserve University in Cleveland, intending to major in mathematics, but he wasn't especially interested in college and had no clear goals. He still wanted to fly airplanes, but there was no way for a black man to become a professional pilot, and Davis realized he was expected to become a professional something. Unfortunately, none of the available professions for blacks—doctor, lawyer, teacher—interested him. And his father's experiences had turned him off the Army.

The elder Davis had always wished he'd gone to the U.S. Military Academy at West Point, and he hoped his son could go. Young men were appointed to West Point by their congressmen, which meant there was almost no chance for a young black man to be appointed. The one black congressman, Oscar De Priest, a representative from the state of Illinois, had appointed a young black man in July 1929, but in December the cadet had been discharged because, like fully one third of the white cadets in his class, he could not keep up with the academic work. Benjamin Davis, Sr., wrote to De Priest to let him know that his son was qualified for appointment to West Point. But anyone De Priest appointed had to be an Illinois resident, so Davis, Jr., moved to Chicago and entered the University of Chicago in the fall of 1930. The idea of attending West Point had become more and more attractive to him; at least it was a goal for which to strive.

Davis received his appointment from De Priest in the late winter of 1931, and a month later he reported to Fort Sheridan, Illinois, for three days of examinations. Since he had already had one and a half years of college and gotten good grades, Davis thought he would have no trouble passing the academic part of the examination. He was surprised at how hard it was and knew he did not do well on the parts covering English history and European history. He was ashamed to tell his father that he had flunked.

However, the official notification that he had failed, which came as no surprise, made him determined to show his family that they could be proud of him. He resolved to get into West Point,

Benjamin O. Davis, Jr., was one of the first Tuskegee airmen in 1943.

graduate from the academy, and join the Army Air Corps.

The academic part of the examination for West Point was given only once a year. Davis took college courses until the end of the fall quarter of 1931, and then began to study hard for the entrance exam. After two months, he was certain he could pass, and he did. He was notified by the War Department to report to West Point on July 1, 1932.

Arriving there, Davis soon discovered that the next four years were going to be extremely lonely ones. While other new arrivals had been assigned roommates, he was placed in a room by himself, because the administration didn't think any of his white classmates would want to room with a black. Worse, he was "silenced" by every other cadet at the academy. "Silencing" meant that no one talked to a cadet except in the line of duty. Usually it was used against students who had violated West Point's code of honor. But in the case of Benjamin Davis, Jr., it was because most of the cadets did not want blacks at West Point.

Traditionally, those black cadets who had not left because of failure to keep up with the academic work had been forced to leave by intimidation. It was a disgrace to the white cadets when Henry O. Flipper managed to become the first black graduate of the academy in 1877; and they were determined that he would not only be the first but also the last. A cadet named Johnson C. Whittaker, who was a former slave from South Carolina, had entered West Point in 1876 and roomed with Flipper his first year. But after Flipper graduated, he roomed alone. When "silencing" Whittaker for four years didn't work, three unidentified cadets wearing masks entered his dormitory room and cut his hair, slashed his ears, beat him, and then tied him to the bed. They warned him, "If you don't get out, we'll cut you like you cut cane as a slave."

After Whittaker reported the incident, instead of searching for his attackers, the administration at West Point accused him of staging the incident to avoid taking a philosophy examination. He was court-martialed and discharged from the academy. Not until 1994, more than a century later, did Whittaker's family's attempts to clear his name (and a book about the racism at West Point that had led to his dishonor) produce legislation in Congress to posthumously commission him an officer in the Army.

Whittaker's was the worst story of abuse of black cadets at West Point in the 1870s and 1880s. Of the twenty-three African-American cadets who attended West Point, only three graduated.

When Benjamin O. Davis, Jr., arrived in the early 1930s, there had been no black graduates since the nineteenth century. When cadets traveled to football games on buses or trains, he had to sit by himself. During the whole four years, he never had a roommate. Nor did he ever have a casual conversation with another cadet. He was, as he later recalled, an "invisible man." But he refused to bow to the pressure and leave West Point. Unhappy as he was, he realized he would be even more unhappy if he let himself be forced out. He did not complain, not even to his parents, for he realized that there was little that could be done without causing trouble. He simply took his father as a role model. The older man had endured a great deal of adversity in the Army and triumphed. He planned to do the same.

Although he had trouble with his course work at first, Davis's grades improved the harder he studied. He also did well in several sports. But he was extremely lonely and looked forward to his furloughs, when he was able to visit his family. During one of these holidays he met Agatha Scott, a beautiful young woman from New Haven, Connecticut, who was attending the Art Institute in that city. If West Point regulations had not banned cadet marriages, he would have married her while still at the academy. He determined to marry her as soon after graduation day as possible. In the meantime, Agatha drove from New Haven to West Point to visit him each Saturday, which made his time at the academy much easier to bear.

During the summer after his junior year, Davis and his classmates received on-site training at Fort Monroe, Virginia; Fort Benning, Georgia; and Mitchell Field, New York. At the forts, Davis learned about infantry as well as field and coast artillery, and found the field and coast artillery intriguing. He was not at all interested in the infantry. The best time of the summer was the five days spent at Mitchell Field. He flew as a passenger in both bombers and observation planes and relived the exhilarating feeling of his first plane ride. He was more convinced than ever that the Army Air Corps was the branch of the service for him. That fall he applied for the U.S. Army Air Corps, easily passing the physical examination.

Soon afterward, however, he was called into the office of the commandant of West Point and handed a letter that said he'd been rejected because no black units were to be included in the Air Corps. Davis was shocked. Angry and hurt, he wondered how

America could possibly call itself the land of the free. But after a while he accepted the rejection and determined to hold on until the policy changed.

The superintendent, General William D. Connor, told Davis that the rejection was only the beginning of many disappointments he would experience in the Army because of his race. It was not "logical" for a black officer to command white troops, he said, and suggested that Davis attend law school so he could later enter politics and have a career as a congressman. But Davis was not interested in either studying law or entering politics. In fact, General Connor's advice had the same effect on him as had his failure the first time he took the West Point entrance exam, and the "silencing" by the other cadets at the academy: It made him stubbornly determined to succeed in spite of the obstacles. He decided to remain in the Army.

In June 1936, Benjamin O. Davis, Jr., became the first African American to graduate from West Point in the twentieth century. He received a lot of press coverage and many letters and telegrams of congratulations. Although he was proud to have accomplished what he had set out to do, Davis's main feeling was one of relief. The past four years had been a grueling experience.

Two weeks after graduation, Benjamin Davis

married Agatha in the Cadet Chapel at West Point. They then set off for Chicago, where Congressman Oscar De Priest awaited them with a full schedule of visits to churches and black social organizations. De Priest wanted to show off his black appointee who had graduated from West Point. Then the couple headed South, to Davis's first posting at Fort Benning, about an hour's drive from Tuskegee Institute, where his father was teaching.

Fort Benning, the largest military installation in the country, was not welcoming to the Davises. He was denied admittance to the Officers' Club, and the commander of the 24th Infantry and his wife did not visit them, as they did as a courtesy to all other new officers. Life was segregated in almost every way. Davis was the only black officer, except for the chaplain. Segregation in the surrounding areas of Georgia and Alabama was even worse, so the couple rarely left the base except to visit Tuskegee.

The only good thing about the year the Davises spent at Fort Benning was that they were together. Professionally, Davis considered it a bust. The all-black unit did very little in the way of training or preparation for combat. Black troops were not expected to fight but to do janitorial jobs.

The first class of black pilots in U.S. history to receive their wings at Tuskegee Institute.

Davis was then assigned to Infantry School at Fort Benning and, after a year there, he was promoted to captain. He then received orders to go to Tuskegee Institute to command the Junior ROTC unit there. Davis worried that, like his father, he would be shuttled back and forth between Tuskegee and Wilberforce (an all-black university in Ohio with an officers' training program) because the Army didn't want him to command white troops.

As the war in Europe intensified, and as relations between the United States and Japan deteriorated, the United States began to gear up for war. In the fall of 1940 President Roosevelt nominated Benjamin O. Davis, Sr., for the rank of brigadier general. The Senate confirmed the nomination, and the senior Davis was assigned command of the 4th Cavalry Brigade, which consisted of the all-black (except for the officers) 9th and 10th Cavalry regiments at Fort Riley, Kansas.

Meanwhile, Captain and Mrs. Davis had barely settled in at Fort Riley when he received the orders he had hoped might someday come: He had been chosen to train for and command the new black flying unit of the U.S. Army Air Corps, activated in March 1941 at Tuskegee Institute.

The Air Corps and Tuskegee rushed to build an airstrip, which ironically was named Moton Field in honor of the late former president of Tuskegee, Robert R. Moton, the same Robert R. Moton who had refused the request of members of the Challenger Air Pilots' Association in Chicago to introduce an aerospace program at Tuskegee a decade earlier. The airstrip was surrounded by a white community that worried about the presence of so

Marjorie Dorsey (left), apprentice mechanic, preparing Cadet Cornelius G. Roger's plane for flight at Tuskegee.

many blacks in uniform, and relations between that community and the black airmen were constantly strained. But while it might have been easier to have integrated black pilots into existing Army Air Corps facilities, the Air Corps had no intention of doing that. If it had to accept black pilots, it intended to segregate them as much as possible from the regular Air Corps.

Benjamin Davis, Jr., was in the first class of thirteen aviation cadets, who were taught by white Army Air Corps instructors. Succeeding classes were taught by black training instructors who were drawn almost exclusively from the pilots who had been trained in the Civilian Pilot Training program. The chief pilot trainer was Charles A. Anderson, of the Anderson-Forsythe team. Since the late 1930s he had been living near Tuskegee and operating his own flight training school with his own Piper Cub airplane.

Others in that first class included two men from active Army artillery units, a policeman, and men with advanced college degrees. They took their training flights in PT-17s, biplanes with strong engines that could withstand a lot of abuse. When Davis was allowed to take one of the planes up by himself, he delighted in doing acrobatics, just as he'd seen at his first air shows in Washington,

DC. The class traveled to Maxwell Field near Montgomery, Alabama, to do night flights, because the Tuskegee airstrip was not equipped with the necessary lighting.

From the PT-17, Davis graduated to the BT-13, a larger plane, and then to the AT-6, which, unlike the other planes, had retractable landing gear so the pilot didn't have to crank the wheels down manually. Davis loved them all, for each one meant he could experience the sheer joy of flying. He was one of five from the original thirteen who completed all the training and received his wings at the graduation ceremony in March 1942.

Following his graduation, Davis was appointed commandant of cadets. In that position, he concentrated on excellence, realizing that war was coming and that if the Tuskegee pilots proved themselves capable in air combat, they would represent a giant leap forward for all African Americans. But he really had little to do, for the cadets were so motivated to excellence that they did not need outside prompting. One member of the Tuskegee airmen was especially motivated: Peter Whittaker, grandson of Johnson C. Whittaker, who had been unfairly discharged from West Point in 1880.

What Davis wanted to do was prove himself in

Benjamin Davis, Jr., in his plane in 1942.

combat, and he kept himself at the ready by frequently checking out the P-40 pursuit aircraft that
he would use in actual combat and in taking practice
flights. But it took some time for the Army Air
Corps, whose name had been changed to Air Force,
to deploy the 99th Fighter Squadron. The Army,

and the War Department, were concerned about the effect an all-black squadron would have on the morale of white pilots and troops, and kept looking for a place in the world where they wouldn't be resented. While waiting for combat orders, Davis was promoted to lieutenant colonel and given a new position, executive for troops.

Finally, in early April 1943, twenty-three pilots, engineers, ground-crewmen, and messmen of the 99th Fighter Squadron commanded by Lieutenant Colonel Davis boarded a train for New York City, where they transferred to a former luxury liner that had been converted for war use. They learned that they were bound for North Africa.

There were many "theaters" or battlefronts in World War II. Often called simply "fronts," they were areas where the Allied forces (England, France, Russia, and the United States) fought for territory against the Axis powers (Germany, Italy, and their allies). North Africa was an important front. There, the troops of the Italian dictator Benito Mussolini, and those of the German general Erwin Rommel, called "The Desert Fox," were trying to gain control. The 99th Fighter Squadron, inexperienced in actual combat, had their first combat experience on that front.

By the time they arrived, British and U.S. forces had come from separate directions to meet and surround Axis forces near Gafsa, Tunisia. They had every intention of driving out the Axis troops but had not as yet done so.

On arrival, the 99th's pilots were issued aircraft at Casablanca and began to engage in "dogfights" with members of the 27th Fighter Group. These "dogfights" were important exercises for both groups, because they gave them practice. The 27th Fighter Group aviators were all white, but there were no racial incidents.

The first day of combat was June 2, 1943, when the 99th's pilots flew a strafing mission over the island of Pantelleria off Sicily, which was still held by the enemy. They also flew escort for other bombers. They met no enemy for the first week. Their first encounter with enemy aircraft took place one week later, on June 9, as members of the 99th were escorting a flight of other bombers on a routine mission. Although the German Me-109s were faster and could fly higher than the P-40s, 99th pilot Willie Ashley managed to damage one of them.

After the surrender of Pantelleria, the area commander, Colonel J. R. Hawkins, wrote to Davis to congratulate the 99th, saying, "You have met the challenge of the enemy and have come out of

Lieutenant Colonel Benjamin Davis, Jr., (on wing), giving final flight instructions to Lieutenant Charles W. Dryden, in 1943.

your initial christening into battle stronger than ever."

Early in July 1943, the 99th participated in the invasion of Sicily. Lieutenants Sherman White and James McCullin were shot down in the fighting. The 99th remained in North Africa and acted as escorts for other combat aircraft. The squadron was then transferred to Sicily. There, in early September,

Davis received word that he would assume command of the 332nd Fighter Group, which included three new squadrons and several support units. It was an all-black unit except for its white commander and white training personnel.

Davis believed that the 99th would continue to do well without him. But when he returned to the United States to take charge of the 332nd Fighter Group, which had yet to be sent into the field, he learned that some in the "top brass" of the Army Air Corps believed that the "Tuskegee Experiment" had failed. Colonel William Momyer of the 33rd Fighter Group wrote a letter saying that the 99th had not been sufficiently disciplined in the air, had not operated satisfactorily as a team, and that its pilots had not been aggressive. The suggestion was that the 99th should be removed from combat duty and assigned to U.S. coastal patrol, a boring assignment since it was unlikely that the United States mainland would be attacked by enemy forces.

On receiving Momyer's report, Henry A. ("Hap") Arnold, the commanding general of the Army Air Force, recommended to General George C. Marshall, the Army Chief of Staff, that the 99th be removed from active combat; that the 332nd Fighter Group, when ready for combat, be sent to a noncombat area; and that a plan to activate a black bombardment group, the 477th, be abandoned.

Davis was furious and certain that the criticisms had nothing to do with the actual performance of the 99th Fighter Squadron and everything to do with the entrenched racism of the Army Air Force and its white officers. But he knew he could not respond to Momyer's criticisms by crying racism. Instead, he called a press conference at the Pentagon, the headquarters for the U.S. military, in Washington, DC, and presented the facts as he knew them: that the 99th had performed as well as any fighter squadron, black or white; that at first they were unused to combat and working as a team, but that they had quickly turned from inexperienced flyers into seasoned veterans. Any early lack of aggression had quickly been made up for as the pilots gained confidence and began to work successfully as a team.

Davis was then called to meet at the Pentagon with the War Department Committee on Special Troop Policies, which had been formed to discuss ways to use black troops. He made a similar presentation there, and took the opportunity to raise the question of training blacks and whites together instead of segregating them, since they would be fighting together in the field.

Davis's defense of the 99th Fighter Squadron was

effective enough to cause General Marshall to order a study of the 99th by the Army operations office. Called "Operations of the 99th Fighter Squadron Compared with Other P-40 Squadrons in the Mediterranean Theatre of Operations," the study concluded that during the eight-month period from July 1943 through February 1944 there was "no significant general difference between this squadron and the balance of the P-40 squadrons in the Mediterranean Theatre Operations."

The 99th Fighter Squadron was not reassigned to coastal duty in the United States.

The charges made by Colonel Momyer had not been proved, and reassignment of the squadron, together with the other recommendations made by General Arnold, were not followed. As previously scheduled, Benjamin O. Davis, Jr., went to Selfridge Army Airfield, near Detroit, Michigan, to assume command of the 332nd Fighter Group, which was composed of the 100th, 301st, and 302nd fighter squadrons.

The 332nd had started out at Tuskegee Airfield and moved to Selfridge in late March 1943. Unlike Tuskegee, Selfridge had both black and white men, and the base had a history of racial tensions, caused mostly by the refusal of the white top brass to grant equal consideration to the black soldiers, but also by the white civilians who lived around the base. Another reason was that the 332nd had not become a team, or group of teams, because there had been so many changes. Officers had been transferred among the three squadrons, enlisted men had arrived. To add to the difficulties, in June 1943 the 332nd was assigned a new airplane, the P-39.

At about the same time, a new white officer, Colonel Robert R. Selway, Jr., took command of the 332nd and began an intensive training program that not only helped the pilots and mechanics learn about the new plane but also helped the men begin to work as a team. By the time Davis arrived in October to take command of the 332nd, many of the earlier problems had been solved.

The P-39 was a fighter plane that the United States' ally, Russia, had used successfully in combat. It was equipped with four, 50-caliber machine guns mounted at the ends of the wings and a 37-millimeter cannon in the hollow propeller hub in its nose. A small combat aircraft, its cockpit was so tiny that the six-foot tall Davis had trouble fitting his legs into it. But the plane was what they had, so he never publicly criticized it.

Davis concentrated on building teams and on selecting competent squadron leaders. He also did what he could to increase the morale of his men by negotiating their admission to the previously all-white post motion picture theater.

The 332nd left for Italy in January 1944 and arrived just days after the most important victories in the short history of the 99th Fighter Squadron.

Black troops in Italy during World War II.

Its pilots proved their fitness for combat with victories in the air over Anzio, in Italy. A total of twelve enemy aircraft were destroyed. Wrote Davis in his autobiography, "There would be no more talk of lack of aggressiveness, absence of teamwork, or disintegrating under fire. The 99th was finally achieving recognition as a superb tactical fighter unit, an expert in putting bombs on designated targets, and a unit of acknowledged superiority in aerial combat with the *Luftwaffe* [German Air Force]."

In March 1944, Davis was recommended for the Legion of Merit medal for his service with the 99th. Coming six months after he had left the 99th, the recommendation was, Davis believed, a sort of apology for the attempts to damage the reputation of the squadron, and of Davis as its commanding officer. Nevertheless, he accepted the award happily because it represented official recognition of the 99th's combat performance.

More official recognition was to come. By May 1944, the 99th had downed a total of 17 enemy planes and was continuing to carry out important dive-bombing missions against vital targets in the Italian campaign. Although the 99th was supposed to have joined the 332nd, General John Cannon asked that the 99th remain in Italy until an intensive bombing operation had been completed in May.

"He regarded the 99th as his most hardened and experienced P-40 unit and wanted it for pinpoint dive-bombing missions close to our frontline troops," wrote Davis in his autobiography. What was even more significant was that General Cannon had, back in 1942, endorsed General Momyer's report about the unsatisfactory performance of the 99th.

The 332nd was assigned to the 62nd Fighter Wing, 12th Air Force, with orders to serve as convoy escorts, harbor protection, reconnaissance, and strafing, among other duties. The port of Anzio was an important strategic target, with supplies constantly coming in, so convoy-escorting and harbor protection were important tasks. During the three months the 332nd was assigned to the 62nd Fighter Wing, they did not see much action, but the pilots gained valuable flying experience. Thus, Davis believed, they were ready for combat.

The 332nd was offered combat reassignment not long after the aerial victories of the 99th Fighter Squadron. They were transferred to the 306th Wing, 15th Fighter Command. Davis was promoted to full colonel.

The job of the 15th Fighter Command was to escort the heavy bombers—B-17s and B-24s—of the 15th Air Force on long missions into Romania, Austria, Germany, France, Spain, and other theaters of the war. The 332nd established itself at Ramitelli, an agricultural area on the shore of the Adriatic Sea, and was soon joined by the 99th, making it a four-squadron fighter group, the largest fighter group in the Italian theater.

The group now switched to the P-47 aircraft, a heavier and more rugged craft than the P-39 with eight .50-caliber machine guns. It was nicknamed "the Jug" because of its size and weight. In early June, 1944, right after the Allied invasion of Normandy (in which U.S. and British troops landed on the coast of France), the 332nd flew penetration escort missions farther into Axis-held territory in Italy.

Developments in fighter craft technology proceeded at great speed in wartime and, after about a month in the P-47s, the 332nd switched to P-51 Mustangs, which had a longer range and performed better at higher altitudes. Because the tails of the craft were painted red, the planes and the 332nd pilots became known as the Red Tails. Colonel Davis led missions in both types of craft, acting as formation leader. By the end of the summer the pilots of the 332nd had established a strong reputation as experts in bomber escort. With the invasion of France and the fall of Rome, morale among the African-American combat pilots was exceptionally high.

African-American war correspondents made sure that the people at home knew how valuable the black pilots were to the war effort. And they used their reports on combat success in the European theater to press the cause of true integration in the military. For, as important as the contributions were of the black pilots and other military men, there was still great reluctance on the part of the military authorities to treat blacks equally.

Back in the United States, the same old habits of segregation continued. White officers without any combat training were more likely to be assigned to train black pilots than were black combat veterans. Reluctance to assign black officers to positions of responsibility over white troops meant that there was a surplus of black officers with little to do at places like Tuskegee Army Airfield.

The attitude of the top brass was expressed by Major General Frank O.D. Hunter, when he visited Selfridge Air Base in April 1944 in response to a War Department investigation of conditions at the base. Hunter met with black officers of the 477th Bombardment Group, which was stationed there, and told them, "This country is not ready to accept a colored officer as the equal of a white one. You are not in the Army to advance your race. Your prime purpose should be in taking your training and fighting for your country and winning the war. In that way you can do a great deal for both your race and your country."

Six months later, the pilots of the 332nd proved that African Americans could die as easily in combat as whites: A total of 15 pilots were lost in the course of missions in the Italian theater in October. The saddened men of the 332nd tried to keep their spirits up with hopes of more decisive victories and an end to the war. But winter weather settled over the Italian theater and increasingly limited flying in the target and base areas by the Allied propeller-driven craft. In December, the men of the 332nd saw their first jet airplanes when German Me-262s attacked their formation. Wrote Davis in his autobiography, "If Hitler had concentrated on building and manning these jet fighters, he could have effectively stopped our bombing operations."

By February, the weather had improved, and air combat missions had increased. The Allied propeller-driven craft actually outdid the German jets in one air battle in March, and the 332nd was awarded the Distinguished Unit Citation for its accomplishments. The unit also received many promotions, and individual pilots were awarded the Distinguished Flying Cross.

The following month, April, the 332nd flew 54 combat missions, more than in any single month previously. They lost several planes and pilots but also shot down 17 enemy aircraft. Ironically, President Franklin D. Roosevelt also died in April, just a month before the war in Europe ended with an

General Benjamin O. Davis decorating his son Colonel Benjamin O. Davis, Jr.

Allied victory. Berlin, the capital of Germany, fell to Allied forces on May 2, and the German forces in Italy surrendered. The war in Europe formally ended on May 8, ever after called V-E (Victory in Europe) Day.

At the end of May, General Benjamin O. Davis, Sr., flew to Italy to personally pin the Distinguished Flying Cross on his son. The older man had not had the opportunity to serve in combat as his son had, but he was proud that the younger man had had such opportunities and distinguished himself.

While awaiting new orders, Davis and the 332nd remained in Italy. They continued training flights and began a program of studying Japanese aircraft, for the war in the Pacific was still going on. In June, Davis and 40 officers and enlisted men boarded two B-17 aircraft for the return trip to the United States. Two months later, with the United States' bombing of Hiroshima and Nagasaki in Japan ordered by the new president, Harry S. Truman, the war in the Pacific ended, and World War II was over at last.

5

WORLD WAR II— THE TRAGEDY

DAVIS's next assignment was to head the troubled 477th Bombardment Group, which had a short but turbulent history.

Once the success of the 99th Fighter Squadron and the 332nd Fighter Group had been established, black leaders in the United States began publicly to express their concern that training black pilots only for single-engine pursuit combat would not prepare them for peacetime aviation. They wanted to see African Americans trained in multi-engine aviation as well. Thus, they campaigned for an all-black bombardment group. The Air Forces' hierarchy bowed to this pressure and created the 477th Bombardment Group in June 1943, but they had no intention of ever deploying it. Rather, they hoped that by the time the new group was ready for combat the war would be over. The Air Force went about the motions so they could not be accused of discrimination.

To be fair, the Army Air Forces had some reasons for not wanting to form an all-black bombardment group in 1943. One was that while blacks had made great strides as pilots, there were not enough trained bombardiers and navigators. To operate a proper bombardment group, these types of personnel were essential.

"By the middle of 1943, 19,637 blacks were in the Army Air Forces," writes Stanley Sandler in his book, *Segregated Skies: All-Black Combat Squadrons of World War II.* "This number was insufficient to draw upon rapidly for personnel for a four-squadron, multi-engine bombardment group, and to supply replacements for the 332nd Fighter Group as well."

Since the Army Air Forces had only recently started to train black bombardiers and navigators, they had to get the needed personnel quickly, and that meant lowering the qualifying test scores. This, of course, opened the way for criticism of African-American personnel as not being well qualified. But it was a no-win situation for both blacks and the Army Air Forces.

To compound the problems, the black men of the 477th had, in general, more education than whites in other bombardment groups. In addition, they were primarily from the North and not used to the discrimination and segregation that southern blacks lived with on a daily basis. Put these conditions in a situation like the Army Air Forces of 1943, whose primarily white population considered blacks inferior even if their test scores had been as high as those of whites, and there was bound to be trouble.

To make matters more difficult, one of those whites happened to be placed in command of the new 477th. Although Colonel Robert R. Selway, Jr. had had successful previous experience commanding black airmen, having served as second commanding officer of the 332nd Fighter Group in its early days, he clearly did not want to be in his new job and did not believe the experiment could work.

Besides a poor choice of commanding officer, the home base for the training of the men of the new 477th was a bad one: Selfridge Field near Detroit, Michigan, had experienced a recent spate of racial incidents, including a case in which three black officers had attempted to enter the base officers' club and been personally barred from the club by the base's commander.

Underlying the racial problems at Selfridge were fears on the part of the surrounding white community that an influx of blacks at the base would aggravate troubles with the city of Detroit, whose

Lieutenant Clarence Lester (right), who shot down three Nazi planes in one mission.

black population was increasing steadily during the war. Among those fears was that black "outside agitators" from Detroit were inspiring blacks on the base to revolt.

Not long after the 477th set up at Selfridge, the group received orders to move to Godman Army Air Field in Kentucky, while the 553rd Fighter Squadron, which had been organized to train replacements for the 477th, was moved to Walterboro Field in South Carolina. Almost immediately, there were problems at both bases, and the 477th and 553rd were moved again. In less than a year the various units of the group made thirty-eight moves, which of course seriously disrupted their training.

The last move during that period was to Freeman Field in Indiana. Colonel Selway had made detailed plans for life at Freeman Field for the men of the 477th. Each building at the field was labeled by race, and there were two specially designated officers' clubs for blacks. In doing so, he directly countermanded War Department directives that, while allowing racial segregation by unit, prohibited segregation in common facilities.

Almost immediately, both enlisted men and officers of the 477th began to challenge the racial segregation, not only on the base but in the surrounding community. A group of enlisted men

The Army Air Force 477th Bombardment Group.

and one officer attempted to obtain service at a restaurant in a nearby town. On base, small groups of black officers tried to gain admittance to the white officers' club, while the men of the officers' club designated for blacks elected a white officer to their board.

On April 5, 1945, a group of about one hundred men from a combat-crew training squadron arrived from Godman Field. Having learned of the segregation at Freeman Field, they were prepared to challenge it immediately. That very evening four black officers attempted to enter the white officers' club. Denied admittance, they left. But half an hour later, nineteen more black officers pushed past the guard at the door and entered the club. The club officer

Aviation cadets preparing for flight at Tuskegee Air Field.

arrested them and ordered them taken back to their quarters. Approximately an hour later, fourteen more black officers entered the club and were arrested. About fifteen minutes after that, three black officers forced their way into the club and were arrested. The following afternoon, twenty-four black officers entered the club and were also arrested. Later that afternoon, Colonel Selway ordered the white officers' club closed.

Then, on the advice of the Air Forces' legal counsel, Colonel Selway issued a regulation that all officers on base were to sign. It stated that the two officers' clubs on base were really one and that due to circumstances they were temporarily separate. While the regulation was clearly a lie, most officers recognized it as a quick way to restore peace through Air Force authority. All the white officers and most of the black officers signed it. But 101 black officers, representing practically all of the 477th Combat Command Training Squadron plus about 20 men from the 619th Bombardment Squadron, refused to sign it.

The following day, each of these men was individually read the 64th Article of War that prohibited the disobeying of a direct order by a superior officer in wartime, on threat of court-martial. Each was then given a direct order to sign Colonel Selway's

Cadets at Tuskegee, 1942, being instructed in sending and receiving Morse code.

regulation. As each refused, he was arrested. Then all 101 were transported by air to Godman Field and put in lockup. For committing a wartime capital offense, all of the men faced court-martial and possible execution.

In response to the resulting hue and cry from the black community, a number of Congressmen and

Senators made official inquiries about the matter. An official investigation was undertaken, and the conclusion was that the base command had gone against Army Air Force's regulations in the first

Army Air Corps aviators, using model planes, practice flight maneuvers.

place by specifying segregated officers' clubs. In the end, all but the three black officers who had used force to enter the white officers' club were released. Of the three held for trial, two were acquitted and one was convicted of using force and fined a modest sum of money.

Shortly after these trials, which took place in July 1945, Colonel Selway was relieved of his position as commanding officer of the 477th and was replaced by Colonel Benjamin O. Davis, Jr.

The following month, President Franklin Delano Roosevelt died, Vice President Harry S. Truman succeeded to the presidency, and Nazi Germany surrendered, ending the war in Europe. The major victory of 101 black officers who had challenged segregation in the Army Air Forces at the risk of death was overshadowed by those larger events. Their victory was not widely reported, even in the black press; and they had to be content with the knowledge that they had stood on personal principles and won.

The 477th never did see combat. With the war in Europe over, there was no point in sending them across the Atlantic. Plans to put them into the Pacific war stalled when some commanding officers in that theater argued that their presence would "complicate" the U.S. effort. Plans to disband the unit and place its personnel in other units also met with resistance on the part of various commanding officers who were concerned that the demonstrated "rebelliousness" of the group would lead to problems elsewhere. The 477th remained together as a unit until 1947, but in spite of Colonel Benjamin Davis's attempts to raise its morale, it was probably the unit least committed to the United States Air Force. Its men had been through too much to have any interest in remaining in the service; most were just marking time until their tours of duty were up. The end of the war was a relief for them, as well as for the armed service that could not figure out what to do with them.

While the 477th Bombardment Group never saw combat, the method of protest its officers chose to use foretold the types of protest used in the civil rights movement in the 1950s and 60s. They were pioneers in the stand taken by blacks later on: that they would no longer accept the indignities of segregation. The 477th had been moved a total of 38 times in its first year of existence and a group of its officers had forcibly integrated a segregated officers' club and risked death for this wartime act of insubordination.

Under Davis's command, the 477th was moved yet again, this time to Lockebourne Army Air Field in Ohio in March 1946. The 477th now became a Tactical Air Command installation with the threefold task of demobilization, recruitment of military personnel, and maintenance of combat readiness. Tuskegee Army Airfield was closed down in 1946, and its pilots who wanted to stay in the service were reassigned to Lockebourne. Soon, the 477th was reorganized again, becoming the 332nd Fighter Group and then, in August 1947, in response to another reorganization, part of the 332nd Fighter Wing. One month before, the Army Air Forces had become an independent service, the United States Air Force (USAF).

6

INTEGRATION

WITH World War II over, the various branches of the U.S. military faced the tremendous task of demobilizing thousands and thousands of men, women, and machines. While it was important that the nation be ready for future wars, it was not cost-effective or efficient to maintain a huge, peacetime military.

Many men and women in the military wanted to return to civilian life. But others had found what they considered real careers in the military and realized that life in the service enabled them to receive more training, greater job security, and better health benefits than civilian jobs could offer. This was true of many blacks who had served in the military during World War II. Their friends and relatives, not to mention casual acquaintances, saw how well they had done and decided the military might be a good place for them. Favorable press coverage of black contributions to the war effort had caused young black men to feel that the military was a place in which they could distinguish themselves. Immediately after the war, the U.S. military found itself needing to demobilize and yet also with an unprecedented number of black enlistees. So great was the number of black enlistments, in fact, that the Army Air Forces suspended black enlistments entirely for a time in mid-1946.

The question of what to do with black personnel in the postwar period was an important one to the military hierarchy. It was also a complicated one. Many communities where military bases were located, especially in the South, made it known that they would not welcome black personnel. The military itself continued to hold to the opinion that no white personnel should be commanded by a black officer. The number of black units remained small by comparison to white units, meaning that there would be a surplus of black officers. Given that condition, the top brass were reluctant to replace black officers with white ones, even though a man like Benjamin O. Davis, Jr., was past due for assignment to a senior Army Air Forces school, without which he could not be promoted further.

As early as the spring of 1945, the War Department Advisory Committee on Special (formerly

Negro) Troop Policies headed by John J. McCloy had started collecting reports on the functioning of blacks in the war in Europe. Most of the reports by whites reflected the racism of their authors and concluded that blacks did not have intelligence, initiative, or judgment equal to whites. Most did not take into account the fact that blacks on the whole had not had opportunities for education, training, or experience equal to those of their white counterparts. Colonel Robert R. Selway, Jr., who had commanded the 477th Bombardment Group before Colonel Benjamin O. Davis took over, wrote a very damaging report that reflected both his own racism and the problems he'd had with the 477th's officers. He strongly recommended that "there be no Negro flying with the postwar Army Air Forces."

The only positive report from a white officer was that of Colonel Noel Parrish, commanding officer of Tuskegee Army Airfield. Colonel Parrish made a strong case against segregation, saying that in the future the AAF must treat blacks as individuals rather than as members of a race, and that "Negro officers should either be assigned according to qualifications or dismissed." Colonel Parrish pointed out that maintaining segregation, especially in the case of black officers, was inefficient.

In all the war, there had been just one case of

General Benjamin O. Davis with his son, Colonel B.O. Davis, Jr., at a 1943 War Department press conference.

real integration: In the infantry, late in the war, integrated combat riflemen platoons had been formed and were highly successful. Still, this was a basis for hope that integration could work elsewhere in the military.

The staff of the War Department read all the reports and heard further testimony from witnesses for both sides. Among the African-American witnesses called were General Benjamin O. Davis, Sr., and Colonel Benjamin O. Davis, Jr. The Department concluded in a report that blacks in the postwar military should be assigned as individuals. While the report was only a recommendation, and not an official directive, it signaled the trends at the highest government levels.

In July 1947, the United States officially recognized the importance of aviation in the military by making Army Air Forces an independent service called the United States Air Force. The following spring the USAF began yet another study of racial segregation and concluded that integration was more efficient. Still, integration did not become official policy.

Nineteen forty-eight was an election year, and President Harry S. Truman was facing an uphill battle for reelection. Many in his own Democratic Party were against him, especially southern conservatives, and he realized he had nothing to lose by deliberately courting the black vote. On July 26 he issued Executive Order No. 9981, establishing the President's Committee on Equality of Treatment and Opportunity in the Armed Forces, known later as the Fahy Committee.

President Harry S. Truman, in 1947, receiving the proposal to abolish segregation in the Army.

Some top military men greeted the president's order with relief, for they could now proceed to integrate the military, and if it didn't work it wouldn't be their fault. The Army, with the greatest numbers of blacks, seemed to have the hardest time. From the spring of 1948 to early 1950, the Army suspended all black enlistments. U.S. entry into the Korean conflict ended that policy, but still, integration of the Army would be quite long and drawn out.

In the U.S. Air Force the experience was different. The new Secretary of the Air Force, Stuart Symington, had been convinced of the need for integration as far back as 1944. The contributions of the 99th Fighter Squadron and the 332nd Fighter Group had further assured him that integration could work. In early 1949 Symington told President Truman, who had won his bid for reelection the previous November, that his plan was to eliminate segregation completely.

The 332nd was the first all-black unit to be integrated into the larger Air Force. According to the plan, all black officers had to go before a screening board presided over by Colonel Benjamin O. Davis, Jr. All enlisted men took a variety of written tests and were judged according to the scores on their tests, interviews with counselors, past performance, specialty qualifications, and career choices.

Some of the black officers complained about these procedures, arguing that no white officers had to go through such screening to determine if they were fit to serve in an integrated service. But the screening continued, and by May 1950 there were only a few remaining segregated units.

The experience of World War II had a major impact on the movement for black equality in the United States. Black military men had distinguished themselves fighting for their country, and most Americans realized that the very racism the United States had fought against in Europe—Hitler's Nazism—was not so different from racism at home. Returning black veterans, having enjoyed the comparative lack of discrimination in Europe, were not about to put up with second-class citizenship in their own country. Black activists and their white supporters began to press for change. In 1955, blacks in Montgomery, Alabama, boycotted the city buses after a woman named Rosa Parks was arrested for refusing to give up her seat to a white man. Mrs. Parks, as secretary to the local branch of the NAACP, had documented many reports of assaults against black men in uniform.

Martin Luther King, Jr., shown giving his famous "I Have a Dream" speech in Washington, D.C., in 1963.

During the Montgomery bus boycott, a young Baptist minister named Martin Luther King, Jr., rose to prominence. Excited by the possibilities of nonviolent social protest the successful bus boycott represented, King formed the Southern Christian Leadership Conference (SCLC) and began a campaign for voting rights. By 1960, black college students had begun sitting-in for the right to eat at segregated lunch counters. There followed several years of marches and demonstrations across the South that led to important federal legislation, beginning with the Civil Rights Act of 1964 and the Voting Rights Act of 1965. By the late 1960s, the legal underpinnings for equality in all aspects of American life were in place. But laws do not change the minds and hearts of people. That is a process of education that continues to this day.

For the rest of his military career, Benjamin O. Davis, Jr., remained unique. As he put it in his autobiography, "For years after integration became part of Air Force life, we remained 'the only ones.' "

In 1949, Davis received a long overdue assignment to the Air War College, based at Maxwell Air Force Base in Montgomery, Alabama. Without study at the War College, he could not be eligible for further promotion; so he and Agatha, accepting the need to return to the still-segregated Deep

South in order to advance his career, braced themselves for the fact that Davis would be the only black officer stationed at Maxwell. It was hardly the first "first" for Davis, and certainly not the last.

For the most part, the ten months the Davises spent at Maxwell were happy ones. There were a few incidents of discrimination both on the field and off, but in general they were treated well. In his classes, Davis felt equal to his fellow students, and received high marks when his studies were completed.

Davis's next posting was to the Pentagon, U.S. military headquarters in Washington, DC. He would serve there as a staff planning officer within the Directorate of Operations of the U.S. Air Force. He was scheduled to take up his duties in the middle of July after he and Agatha enjoyed a much needed vacation in California. They were in Los Angeles on June 25, 1950, when North Korea invaded South Korea. Within two days, the United States had entered the conflict on the side of South Korea, formally known as the Republic of Korea. Davis felt uncomfortable being on vacation when a war was going on in the Pacific, and Agatha agreed when he proposed to cut short his leave. They left for Washington, DC, and Davis reported for duty a week earlier than scheduled.

Over the next two decades, Davis held several important positions, including Chief of Staff, United Nations Command; the second highest position in the U.N. military. He retired in 1970 at the age of 57, with the rank of permanent major general. In 1991 he published his autobiography, which he entitled *Benjamin O. Davis, Jr., American.*

Even after Davis's retirement, equality in the military remained an elusive goal. The aim of the U.S. Air Force was for a service with a ten percent black population, which reflected the proportion of African Americans in the larger population. By 1971 the Air Force had reached that goal among enlisted men. But lingering racism in the service, which reflected that in the larger society, had prevented a similar proportion of blacks from becoming officers in the Air Force. In 1971, black officers represented only 1.7 percent of the officer total. Nevertheless, blacks had managed to integrate just about all levels of the service. In 1974, Captain Lloyd Newton became the first black pilot to join the elite USAF Demonstration Squadron, called the Thunderbirds.

Many blacks who had gained experience and skill in aviation during World War II had the opportunity to serve in the Korean War during the 1950s and the war in Vietnam in the 1960s. Daniel "Chappie"

Colonel Daniel "Chappie" James in the cockpit of his plane at a base in Thailand.

James, Jr., flew many combat missions in Korea and Vietnam and became America's first black four-star general. In 1975, the same year he was awarded his fourth star, he was named Commander in Chief of the North American Air Defense Command.

Not only did blacks serve in the U.S. Air Force but also in the aviation units of other services, such as the U.S. Navy. Ensign Jesse L. Brown was the first black naval aviator. His plane was struck as he flew a support mission in the Korean War and Ensign Brown died. Posthumously, he was awarded the Distinguished Flying Cross, Air Medal, and Purple Heart. In 1973, an escort ship was named in his honor.

U.S. Army helicopter pilot Captain Ronald A. Radcliffe served heroically in the war in Vietnam and in 1972 was named Army Aviator of the Year.

It has often been said that while the military reflects the larger society, in matters of racial equality it has been in the forefront of changes in America. This was true in the post-World War II era. Despite continuing racism, the military aviation services had a far better record of integration than general aviation.

While white pilots who left the military had some assurance of getting jobs in the growing commercial airline industry, black pilots had few opportunities in this area. One who managed to find a job was Perry H. Young, Jr., who was a flight instructor at the Coffey School of Aeronautics and later a civilian flight instructor at Tuskegee Army Air Field during World War II. After the war, he got his helicopter pilot's license and in 1956 was hired by New York Airways, which operated a ferry service between several suburban airports and a heliport in New York City. Perry Young spent 22 years with that company and then moved to New York Helicopter as chief pilot.

In the case of most black pilots, if they wanted to remain in aviation, they had to start their own aviation businesses. This was true of James O. Plinton, Jr., who like Young had served as a civilian flight instructor at Tuskegee Army Air Field in World War II. In 1948 Plinton and Maurice De Young founded Quisqueya, Ltd., a Caribbean airline that operated between Haiti and the Turks and Caicos Islands. After that small airline folded, Plinton became one of the few blacks to hold executive positions with major commercial airlines. Between 1957 and his retirement in 1979, Plinton held important posts with Trans World Airlines and Eastern Airlines.

Those with the fortitude to do so went to court to protest discrimination in commercial aviation. When Marlon D. Green was denied employment with Continental Airlines, he sued on the basis of

Jill E. Brown was the first black woman to fly as a pilot for a major U.S. airline.

racial discrimination. After a long court battle, he won his case in 1965 and became a Continental Airlines pilot. His successful suit set a precedent and influenced other commercial airlines to review their hiring practices. As a result, other blacks began to find employment with major airlines.

7

THE SPACE AGE

FOR as long as humans have understood that there is a whole world beyond the sky, they have dreamed of reaching outer space in flying machines that are called spacecraft. World War II saw great advances in aircraft and the understanding of the dynamics of flight. Theories of space mechanics were developed that went beyond science fiction, as well as a small new field called aerospace engineering that was investigating the possibilities of sending craft, manned and unmanned, into orbit around the earth and beyond. Scientists in the Soviet Union, which had been an ally of the United States during World War II, were working hard on an artificial earth satellite. Scientists in the United States were doing similar work.

The world entered the space age in 1957, when the Soviet Union launched *Sputnik I*, the first unmanned spacecraft. The 184-pound capsule managed to achieve earth orbit and circled Earth for several months. Scientists in the United States were excited by the Soviet achievement. The United States government was very worried about it.

In the decade or so after the end of World War II, the United States had come to see the Soviet Union, with its communist type of government, as a threat to democracy. The two nations entered a "Cold War," in which they did not fight each other with weapons but vied with each other for influence in parts of the world that might be won over to their respective types of government. The term "Third World" was coined after the Second World War to describe countries in Africa, Asia, and elsewhere that might adopt either communism or democracy.

Thus, when the Soviet Union launched the first artificial satellite, the United States government regarded that "first" as a blow to democracy and a victory for communism. Very quickly, the government of the United States made the small U.S. space program a priority. Money was poured into aerospace research and engineering. Educational institutions on all levels were encouraged to increase their teaching of math and science, with the idea

Astronaut John Glenn preparing for space flight in 1962.

that the United States must quickly catch up to and surpass the Soviet Union in space. The term "space race" was coined to describe this competition.

THE SPACE AGE

For the next few years, the United States played catch-up in the space race. President John F. Kennedy, elected in November 1960, made the space program a top priority. The Soviet Union continued to make progress and sent the first human into space in 1961. Yuri Gagarin, whom the Soviets called a cosmonaut, orbited the earth in the Russian spacecraft *Vostok 1*. By 1961, however, the United States had made great strides in developing its space program. On May 5, 1961, just 23 days after Yuri Gagarin was launched into space, the United States sent up its first manned rocket. Commander Alan Shepherd's flight in *Freedom 7* lasted just 15 minutes, and he did not even try to achieve orbit; he simply went up and then came back down. But it was progress nevertheless, and Americans were proud. The following year, in February, Colonel John H. Glenn, Jr., made another historic flight when he became the first American to orbit Earth in *Friendship 7*.

Although public interest in the space program centered around the men (there were no women) who had or would venture into space, the program was staffed by hundreds of technical, scientific, and engineering personnel. By 1962, that group of support personnel included one black American. The man was Dr. Vance H. Marchbanks, Jr., an Air Force flight surgeon and former member of the 332nd Fighter Group, who served on the mission flight control team. As Colonel Glenn orbited Earth, Dr. Marchbanks monitored his heartbeat, respiration, and other vital signs.

In 1963, the year following Colonel Glenn's historic flight, the Air Force astronaut selection board nominated Captain Edward J. Dwight, Jr., for the manned space flight training program. But Captain Dwight was passed over when the final selection was made and left the space program shortly thereafter. The Air Force claimed that Dwight had not completed his training. But Dwight later explained that he resigned under pressure: "They didn't want black involvement," he stated. "They felt that to send blacks into space would lessen the general public's enthusiasm for the space program."

In 1967, Air Force Major Robert H. Lawrence, Jr., was selected as an astronaut in the Department of Defense's Manned Orbiting Laboratory Program. Lawrence's credentials were impeccable: He was a pilot and a scientist with a doctorate in nuclear chemistry. Sadly, Major Lawrence died in a tragic airplane accident later that same year.

While by 1966 the direct-action civil rights movement had achieved major victories in the fight against racial segregation in the South—including important federal laws such as the Civil Rights Act of 1964 and the Voting Rights Act of 1965—the minds and hearts of many white Americans still had not been changed. Although more blacks were

Major Robert H. Lawrence, Jr., standing in front of an Air Force jet.

Astronaut Sally Ride was the first American woman in space.

hired as support personnel over the next decade or so, the astronaut program remained exclusively white and excusively male. It was white male Americans who walked on the moon and scored the other U.S. "firsts" in space.

In July 1969, Neil Armstrong and Edwin ("Buzz") Aldrin landed on the moon in an Apollo spacecraft. During the 1970s, the United States continued manned space explorations in an earth-orbiting space station called Skylab. But after 1972 most space exploration was done by unmanned craft. The main reason was that the planned missions were of such great length that humans could not have lasted until the end. Also, space science had not progressed to the point where anyone knew how long humans could survive in space. It was unmanned spacecraft that scored the major U.S. "firsts" in the early 1970s—*Pioneer 10* became the first man-made object to escape from the solar system in 1973, and the following year *Pioneer 11* photographed Jupiter's moons. The Viking program searched for life in outer space. The Mariner program studied Venus and Mars.

Finally, in 1978, the first woman, Dr. Sally K. Ride, a physicist, and three black men were accepted into the astronaut program. Dr. Guion S. Bluford, Jr., held a doctorate in aerospace engineering. Charles F. Bolden was a graduate of the U.S. Naval Academy, had an MS degree in systems management, and had served as a test pilot at the Naval Air Test Center. Dr. Ronald E. McNair held a doctorate in physics from the Massachusetts Institute of Technology and had worked as a physicist with the Hughes Research Laboratories, part of Hughes Aircraft.

At last the American astronaut program began to reflect the population of the United States. But by this time the American romance with space had dulled. The space program had come to be regarded as too costly, given the results. While the various feats were good for American morale and standing in the world, the general feeling was that the space program needed to fill a practical need if the country was to continue spending huge sums of money on it.

By the time the first woman and the first three black men entered the astronaut program, the focus of the program was on the space shuttle, a reusable spacecraft designed to do practical work in space. Dr. Sally K. Ride became the first American woman in space when she served as one of three mission specialists on the second mission of the space shuttle *Challenger* in June 1983. (The Russians had sent a woman cosmonaut into space way back in 1963, and again in 1982.)

Two months after Dr. Sally Ride's historic flight, Dr. Guion S. Bluford, Jr., became the first African American in space.

Bluford was born in Philadelphia, Pennsylvania, on November 22, 1942. His name is pronounced Guy-on, and he prefers to be called Guy. His father was a mechanical engineer, and from a very young age Guy Bluford was interested in how things work. He was especially interested in airplanes. As a boy, he built model airplanes and collected pictures of real airplanes. He wasn't interested just in the craft but in the way they moved through the air.

Astronaut Guion (Guy) S. Bluford, mission specialist in 1983.

Long before he had ever heard the term "aero-dynamics," Guy Bluford was doing his own experiments. Guy had a paper route, and instead of just tossing the papers onto his customers' front lawns, he practiced different ways of aiming and throwing them. When he played table tennis (sometimes known as Ping-Pong), he practiced different ways of hitting the ball with his paddle. In fact, as a result of his experiments, he became an expert table-tennis player.

By the time Guy Bluford was old enough to think about what he wanted to be when he grew up, he understood that he would go to college. Both his parents had master's degrees and their parents before them had earned college degrees. He also knew that he wanted to study aerospace engineering.

By that time, blacks had made great strides in aviation. If Bluford had wanted to be a pilot, he could have had realistic dreams of doing so. But Bluford was less interested in being a pilot than he was in designing spacecraft. Encouraged by his parents, he finally decided he would study that field in college.

Bluford was fifteen years old and in high school when the Soviet Union launched *Sputnik 1*. As mentioned earlier, the United States government immediately decided that young Americans must be encouraged to excel in science and math and to pursue careers in those fields so the nation could catch up to, and surpass, the Soviet Union in the space race. In speeches and memos the administration of President Dwight D. Eisenhower urged the nation's schools to emphasize the teaching of math and science and to offer encouragement to students who showed an interest in those fields.

But the word apparently didn't reach Guy Bluford's guidance counselor at Overbrook High School in Philadelphia. Bluford was clearly interested in those subjects, but he was not encouraged to go to college. Instead, his counselor told him he was not college material and suggested that he attend a technical school. At a technical school, Bluford could learn computers or become an automobile mechanic, but he could not get an education in aerospace engineering.

Guy Bluford, who says he never had problems with racism or discrimination growing up, gave the guidance counselor the benefit of the doubt, aware that he was not an A student and was a weak reader. Perhaps when Guy Bluford's guidance counselor thought of the space age, he thought only of the straight-A students and did not consider encouraging other students who had aptitudes in science and math.

Guion S. Bluford, onboard the space shuttle *Challenger*.

But too often in the 1950s (and later) white guidance counselors tended to think of blacks as not
capable of academic achievement or professional
careers. Guy Bluford was not the only black youth
who was not encouraged to excel. In fact, for blacks

Bluford's age, being told by white guidance counselors that they were not college material was the rule, not the exception.

But Bluford's parents had raised him and his two younger brothers, Eugene and Kenneth, to believe they could do whatever they wanted to do, as long as they were willing to work hard. So Bluford did not pay much attention to the advice of his high school guidance counselor. There had never been any question in his family that he and his brothers would go to college. In his senior year, he applied to several colleges and, for his senior yearbook, in answer to the question of what he wanted to do with his life, Bluford responded that he wanted to be an aerospace engineer.

Accepted into the aerospace engineering program at Pennsylvania State University, Bluford entered in the fall of 1960, one of only four hundred African-American students among a population of several thousand. Only then did he begin to feel different because he was black. But he did not spend a lot of time worrying about that. He had a busy life with his courses as well as his membership in Air Force ROTC. He enjoyed Reserve Officers Training Corps, and although he could have left the program after his sophomore year, he chose to remain in it, knowing full well that he would be required to serve four years in the Air Force after graduation.

By his junior year, Bluford had become more interested in being a pilot, but he failed a flight physical that year and could not qualify. He could have been a navigator, but he decided to pursue his interest in engineering in the Air Force.

Then, in the summer after his junior year, Bluford attended boot camp at Otis Air National Guard Base in Cape Cod, Massachusetts. There, he again took the flight physical, and this time he passed it. His first ride in an Air Force plane persuaded him that he should become an Air Force pilot after all. In fact, he reasoned, knowing how to fly aircraft would help him be a better aerospace engineer.

Bluford made another major life decision around that time. He decided to get married before finishing college. His bride, Linda Tull, was a fellow student at Penn State.

During his senior year, Bluford enjoyed the status of pilot in the Air Force ROTC and, when he graduated in May 1964 with his BS degree, he also received the ROTC's Distinguished Graduate Award. The following month he became a father when his and Linda's first child, a son whom they named Guion III, was born.

From Penn State, Bluford went immediately into

the Air Force. He and his family moved to Arizona, where he underwent pilot training at Williams Air Force Base. In 1965 he received his pilot wings and almost immediately began a tour of duty in Vietnam.

The civil war between North and South Vietnam was raging by then, and the United States was deeply involved in aiding South Vietnam against the North, which was allied with Communist China. Bluford served with the 557th Tactical Fighter Squadron based in Cam Ranh Bay, South Vietnam. At first, he flew in F-4 jets, and later in F-4C Phantom jets. During his first year in Vietnam, his and Linda's second son, James T., was born. Bluford was unable to be present at the birth, as so often happens to military people in wartime. They set aside their personal lives in order to serve their country.

Guy Bluford served his country with great distinction. During his time in Vietnam, he flew 144 combat missions, 65 of them over enemy territory in North Vietnam. He logged some 3,000 hours of flying time and received ten Air Force medals.

When Bluford returned to the United States, he had to get reacquainted with his wife and young sons. He also had to adjust to noncombat life. The

Air Force had big plans for the man they considered to be one of the best pilots in the service. He was assigned to Sheppard Air Force Base in Texas to teach cross-country and acrobatic flying to other Air Force pilots.

But Bluford had not forgotten his dream of being an aerospace engineer. In 1972 he was accepted at the Air Force Institute of Technology. Two years later he graduated with distinction and with his masters degree in aerospace engineering.

Bluford continued to take courses toward his doctorate at the Air Force Institute of Technology. He also went to work at the Air Force Flight Dynamics Laboratory at Wright-Patterson Air Force Base in Ohio. There, he tested new airplanes and aircraft designs and developed plans for aircraft based on the latest discoveries in aerodynamics. At the laboratory, Bluford studied delta (triangular) wings and developed a computer program that could calculate air pressure, density, and velocity on any part of the wing. That computer program was the basis of the research paper he wrote to complete his doctorate in 1978. The man whose high school guidance counselor had said was not college material had earned the highest academic degree possible in his chosen field.

By the time Bluford was awarded his PhD he had

joined the astronaut program. It seemed to him the best place to combine his interest in flying and in aerospace engineering. He knew it was a long shot to apply to the program, for NASA had cut back its manned-flight program as the public became less interested in spending money on spacecraft and space exploration, and more and more interested in practical applications of the American space program. Also, thousands of people applied to the astronaut program each year. When Bluford applied, he was one of 8,878 would-be astronauts.

Thirty-four men and one woman were accepted into the program in 1978. As mentioned earlier, the group included three blacks, among them Guy Bluford. Sadly, his father, who had died in 1967, did not live to know of his son's achievement. Bluford's mother died in the same year he was accepted, but she lived to share his proud moment.

Guy and Linda Bluford and their two sons moved to Houston, Texas, close to the Johnson Space Center (named after former president Lyndon B. Johnson). Linda got a job with an oil company, and the two boys, who were both now in high school, enrolled in local schools. Guy Bluford also "went back to school," for the first year in the astronaut program was one of intensive study.

First, the astronaut candidates took courses in

shuttle systems, geology, medicine, aerodynamics, communications, and astronomy. Then, they went on a series of field trips to various space centers around the country, including Florida, Alabama, and California. There, they learned as much as they could about the space shuttle program, observing where the craft and the engines were built.

Established in 1972, the space shuttle program aimed to develop reusable spacecraft that could do practical work in space. Part rocket, part spacecraft, and part airplane, shuttles are a unique blend of aerospace engineering knowledge. Rockets are used to propel them, but they have delta wings and can glide on air currents. They are designed to do such work in space as launching communications satellites, building space stations, operating labortories, and launching other craft to the distant reaches of space.

When Guy Bulford joined the astronaut program, the shuttle, after six years, was in its later stages of development. But it would be three years before the first one was launched into space.

At the end of his year in "shuttle school," Guy Bluford became a full-fledged astronaut capable of flying a space shuttle when NASA was ready to launch the first one. To prepare for that eventuality, Bluford and the other shuttle astronauts spent much of their time at Johnson Space Center, and at Rockwell Aircraft Company in California where the shuttles were actually being built. There, they trained in "shuttle simulators," which approximated the conditions of the shuttle in space. What

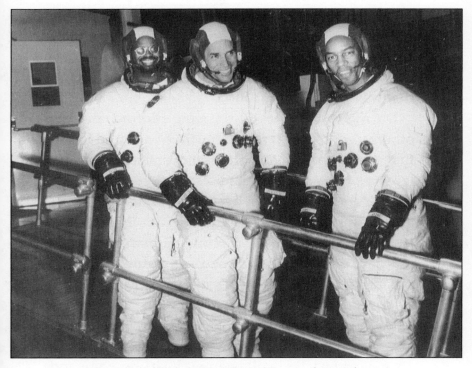

Ronald E. McNair (left), Frederick D. Gregory (center), and Guion S. Bluford (right) training for space shuttle flights at Johnson Space Center.

the simulators could not approximate was the condition of zero gravity, or complete weightlessness, that is only found in space. To get used to zero gravity, the astronauts spent time in a big tank of water called a "water immersion facility," in which they floated and attempted to do the sorts of tasks that they would be called upon to do in the shuttle.

The astronauts also had to learn how to fly the shuttles and practiced making ascents, entries, and controlling the craft in orbit. For someone with a lifelong interest in aerodynamics like Guy Bluford, this was not work but fun.

During these years of training, Bluford and the others understood how special they were and found that their shared specialness overshadowed differences in race and gender. Colonel Frederick Gregory, a black pilot in the United States Air Force, joined the shuttle astronaut program in 1980. Dr. Judith A. Resnik was the second woman to join the program. Dr. Ellison Onizuka became the first Asian American in the program.

At last, in April 1981, the first space shuttle, *Columbia*, was launched with a crew of white males. When it completed its fourth mission on July 4, 1982, its crews had still been exclusively white and male. Then the second shuttle, *Challenger*, was built and ready to be sent into space. Its first flight was in April 1983; for its second flight, in June 1983, Dr. Sally K. Ride was chosen for its crew of three mission specialists.

While one astronaut was mission commander and piloted the shuttle (sometimes with a copilot), the mission specialists performed experiments in space and were experts in the shuttle's operation and cargo, or payload.

Some people wondered why a woman was chosen, rather than an African-American man. But mission specialists on shuttle flights were generally chosen according to their expertise in the particular job to be done, and among the 78 shuttle astronauts the vast majority were white and male. Guy Bluford did not resent the fact that Sally Ride flew in *Challenger* before he did. In fact, he was relieved that she would have to withstand all the media hoopla associated with being a "first," and hoped that by the time his turn came, some of that media interest would have died down.

Lieutenant Colonel Guion Stewart Bluford, Jr.'s, turn came for *Challenger*'s third mission in August 1983. Although he was qualified to pilot the shuttle, he had entered the program as a mission specialist and so would serve in that position. On *Challenger*'s third mission, he would be in charge of deploying a communications and weather satellite for the nation of India. He would also be working on experiments for two American companies that involved separating biological material with electromagnetic waves.

As Bluford had hoped, less media attention was paid to his position as the first American black in space (the Soviet Union had sent Arnaldo Tamayo Méndez, a black Cuban, into space in a *Soyuz 38* spacecraft in 1980) than had been paid to Sally Ride as the first American woman in space. But the nation, and the world, still paid some attention to this "first." President Ronald Reagan, in his message to the crew before liftoff, said, "With this effort, we acknowledge proudly the first ascent of a black American into space."

African Americans were especially proud. Many famous blacks traveled to Cape Canaveral, Florida, to witness the launching. They included the comedian and television star Bill Cosby, who put the event in perspective when he said, "Our race is one which has been quite qualified for a long time. The people who have allowed Guy to make this mission are the ones who have passed the test."

Just before midnight on August 29, 1983, Bluford and his four fellow crew members climbed into the shuttle and were strapped into their seats. A night launch was necessary for this mission because of the payload *Challenger* was carrying. The task of launching the Indian satellite made it necessary both to achieve an orbit different from the orbits of the six earlier shuttle flights.

The crew then went through a series of checks of the various shuttle systems. Some two hours later, as mission control on the ground waited for a severe thunderstorm to pass and the air to clear, the shuttle's auxiliary power units were turned on. At last, a voice from Mission Control shouted "Liftoff!" and, in a blaze of fire and smoke, *Challenger*'s twin solid-fuel boosters lifted the spacecraft from the launchpad. Inside, the crew were amazed at the brightness of the exhaust flames and felt as if they were in the middle of an erupting volcano.

Once *Challenger* had achieved orbit some 200 miles above Earth, the crew set about doing the work they had been trained for—in conditions of zero gravity. That took some adjusting to. Only by looking at objects not in motion could the five men tell if they were upside down or right side up. During daylight hours, they slept wearing eyeshades. The second night, they did some of the biological experiments. The third night they launched the Insat-1B satellite for India, ejecting it above the Pacific Ocean just as the sun was setting.

Bluford was the mission specialist most responsible for the launching of the satellite. He and other members of the crew set the satellite spinning outside the open doors of the shuttle's cargo bay. Approximately 45 minutes later, its own rocket boosters propelled it 22,300 miles above the earth, where it went into orbit. Bluford reported to Mission Control at Cape Canaveral, "The deployment was on time, and the satellite looks good."

President Reagan placed a special telephone call to the shuttle. He praised all the members of the crew but had a special message for Guy Bluford: "You, I think, are paving the way for others, and you are making it plain that we are in an era of brotherhood here in our land."

Soon after midnight on September 5, as *Challenger* passed over the Indian Ocean on its ninety-eighth orbit, the two pilots slowed down the shuttle by firing its two orbital maneuvering engines. The shuttle descended into a lower orbit, then entered Earth's atmosphere and made its way to the coast of California. Gliding toward the runway of Edwards Air Force Base, its landing wheels lowered, and the craft touched down as smoothly as a regular airplane. Its historic flight had ended, and Guion S. Bluford, Jr., had a place in history.

For the next few weeks, he was besieged with requests for interviews and photographs, but after a time the attention died down. Bluford was glad to be just another astronaut again. But of course he was not just another astronaut; he was a role model for young African Americans who dreamed of becoming astronauts themselves. He had done it, and so they knew they could, too.

The shuttle program seemed to be proving that NASA could indeed justify the millions spent by building reusable spacecraft that could do practical work in space. Then, on its fifth mission, *Challenger* burst into flames just after liftoff, and seven Americans perished. They included the first American who was not an astronaut or payload specialist, the first Teacher-in-Space, Christa McAuliffe. Also included were mission specialists Ellison Onizuka and Judith Resnik, payload specialist Greg Jarvis, commander Francis "Dick" Scobee, and pilot Mike Smith. And, the group who gave their lives in the American space program included the second African American in space, Ronald McNair.

Dr. McNair was only thirty-five years old on January 28, 1986, when *Challenger's* equipment failed.

The fatal space shuttle *Challenger* crew members: (front row from left) Michael J. Smith, Francis R. Scobee, and Ronald E. McNair; (back row from left) Ellison S. Onizuka; Sharon Christa McAuliffe, Gregory Jarvis, and Judith A. Resnik.

An O-ring seal on one of the solid rocket booster segment joints failed in the unusually cold weather at Cape Canaveral in Florida. The broken seal allowed flame to escape, burning a hole in the external fuel tank and creating a leak of liquid propellant. The faulty solid rocket booster then broke loose from its attachment and crashed into the tank. As McNair's parents, wife, and two young children looked on from the spectators' gallery at Cape Canaveral, the man they loved and were so proud of perished, surrounded by the belongings he had brought along for the ride, his North Carolina A&T banner, his dark glasses, and his beret.

The *Challenger* disaster threw NASA and the space shuttle program into a turmoil. Only after months of investigation was the problem that had caused the tragedy revealed. Steps were taken to ensure that it would not occur again.

In late November 1989, Air Force Colonel Frederick D. Gregory, who had joined the shuttle program in 1978, became the first African-American mission commander when the shuttle *Discovery* undertook its mission. It was Gregory's second shuttle mission. Two years later he commanded the forty-fourth mission flown in the U.S. shuttle program in *Atlantis*. The mission was a completely military one, with the job of deploying a missile-detection satellite for the Department of Defense and observing military installations on the ground. During the mission, Colonel Gregory had to change the shuttle's orbit in order to avoid hitting part of a discarded Soviet rocket.

In late March 1992, aboard *Atlantis*, the mis-

Astronaut Frederick D. Gregory, mission commander, in the space shuttle *Atlantis.*

sion commander was another African American, Colonel Charles F. Bolden, a graduate of the U.S. Naval Academy, who had joined the shuttle program in 1980. Bolden was making his third shuttle flight. This mission was the first of several planned for the 1990s to study chemical and physical processes at work in Earth's atmosphere and the effects of solar energy on the atmosphere. Among other tasks, they photographed ultraviolet radiation

Shuttle astronauts (from left to right), Lieutenant Colonel Guion S. Bluford, Dr. Ronald E. McNair, Colonel Frederick D. Gregory, and Major Charles F. Bolden.

reflected by the ozone layer and observed ultraviolet light from distant constellations.

At last, in September 1992, aboard the *Endeavour*, the first African-American woman was launched into space: 35-year-old mission specialist Dr. Mae C. Jemison, a physician and chemical engineer.

Born in Chicago in 1957, Mae Jemison knew as

early as kindergarten that she wanted to be a scientist. She also experienced a lack of support at school similar to that Guion Bluford had found in high school. When she told her teacher she wanted to be a scientist, the teacher corrected her: "You mean a nurse," the teacher said. But Mae Jemison found the support she needed at home. Her parents, Charley and Dorothy Jemison, told their three children that they could be whatever they wanted to be. In whatever she wanted to do, whether it was science projects, or dance, or art lessons, "They would find the money, time, and energy to help me be involved," Jemison recalls.

On graduation from high school, Jemison enrolled at Stanford University in California and earned a bachelor's degree chemical engineering. She then entered in Cornell Medical School in Ithaca, New York. While a student there, she went to Thailand and Kenya, bringing much-needed medical knowledge and care to indigent people. On graduation from Cornell with her medical degree, she joined the Peace Corps and served as a staff physician in West Africa.

Following her stint in the Peace Corps, Mae Jemison settled in Los Angeles, California, and opened a general practice in 1985. But she had dreamed since childhood of being an astronaut,

In September 1992, Mae C. Jemison became the first African-American woman in space.

and she also applied for the astronaut program. The fact that there were no black women astronauts did not concern her: "I never did believe there were these differences," she explains, referring to racial and sexual stereotypes. "I always assumed I would go into space ever since I was a little girl. I would have applied to be an astronaut if there had never been a single person in space."

She did not make it into the astronaut program, which must reject many candidates for every one it accepts, even though they are well qualified. Undaunted, she was determined to apply again.

In 1986 the *Challenger* disaster occurred, but that did not faze Dr. Jemison. As a scientist, she understood that problems could occur with new technology. She reapplied to the program in 1987 and this time was one of fifteen new astronauts chosen out of 2,000 applicants.

For the next four years, Jemison trained and studied and prepared for the time when she would go up into space as she had dreamed of doing as a child. When her opportunity came, it was on a mission whose entire focus was scientific experiments. The payload included fish, frogs, and hornets; and the experiments conducted in space included raising tadpoles and comparing their behavior in space with that of tadpoles that had been hatched on

Earth and brought into space. They recorded the brain waves of carp to determine if zero gravity affected the fish's sense of balance. Yet another experiment was to determine if hornets would build nests in zero gravity. Unfortunately, most of the hornets died because of high humidity in their chamber, and those that lived built no nests.

Of the 54 experiments conducted, more than half had been devised by Japanese scientists, and the Japanese government had helped finance the mission. Also, a Japanese citizen was aboard as payload specialist.

By this time, the idea of African Americans in space was no longer new, and while the "first" aspects of Dr. Jemison's flight were not overlooked, she did not have to undergo the same glare of media attention as Guion Bluford or Sally Ride had before her. That was fine with Jemison, who believes that advances in technology are of benefit to African Americans. She believes that the space program particularly holds much promise for blacks: "This is one time when we can get in on the ground floor."

8

THE FUTURE

As Dr. Mae Jemison says, the space program is a field of aviation that developed during a time when African Americans were enjoying greater opportunities to compete equally with whites. As a result, they have made important contributions to it. It is hoped that this situation will hold true in the case of future technological advances in aviation. Space stations operated by humans, colonies in outer space, and other things that are now only possible in science fiction may one day exist; and if African Americans continue to earn advanced degrees in science, mathematics, and engineering, there is no reason why they should not help bring those advances into existence in at least equal proportion to their numbers in the population.

But looking to the future does not mean forgetting the past, and the story of blacks throughout the history of aviation is still too little known.

Entire books on blacks in the military have been written without one mention of blacks' contributions to military aviation. The same is true of published African-American almanacs, heavy volumes of black history that purport to cover all aspects of black life but make no mention of the important history of black aviation.

That deficiency is slowly being addressed. With the increased interest in black history that began in the 1960s and 70s, new generations of Americans discovered Bessie Coleman. A Bessie Coleman Aviators Club was founded in the Chicago area in 1977, and in 1990 a road at Chicago's O'Hare Airport was renamed Bessie Coleman Drive. In 1992, Chicago celebrated its first "Bessie Coleman Day." That same year, she was inducted into the International Women's Sports Hall of Fame as a "pioneer." The woman who read the induction citation was a pioneer in another area, Mrs. Rosa Parks, the woman whose arrest started the Montgomery, Alabama, bus boycott in 1955 that led to the civil rights movement. In 1993, *Queen Bess*, the first full-length biography of Bessie Coleman, by Doris Rich, was published.

But Dr. Mae Jemison, who like Bessie Coleman grew up in Chicago, had never heard of Coleman until 1992 when she saw an exhibit on Coleman at the DuSable Museum of African American History in that city. Jemison recalls in the afterword of *Queen Bess*, "I was embarrassed and saddened that I did not learn of her until my space flight beckoned on the horizon. In fact, I felt cheated." But, on reflection, Jemison decided that knowledge of Bessie Coleman, even coming as late as it did to her, was a gift that "fills me with sunshine, enthusiasm, daring, courage, sadness, hope, joy, triumph, and a firm grip on reality."

Since the early 1980s, the Smithsonian Institution in Washington, DC, has focused national and international attention on the accomplishments of African-American aviation pioneers. In 1982, the Smithsonian's National Air and Space Museum opened an exhibition entitled "Black Wings: The American Black in Aviation." The Smithsonian Institution Press published *Benjamin O. Davis, Jr., American; Queen Bess; Daredevil Aviator*; and other books on blacks in aviation.

In 1994, the Smithsonian Institution Press issued *Loving's Love*, the autobiography of Neal V. Loving. Little-known outside aviation circles, Loving was born in Detroit in 1916 and suffered the same barriers to his dream of becoming an aviator as other blacks of his time. But he overcame those barriers, learned to fly, and built his first flying machine as

Astronaut Mae C. Jemison in zero gravity in the space shuttle *Endeavour.*

a young high school graduate. In 1944 he was in a glider accident and lost both his legs. But just six years later he unveiled and flew *Loving's Love,* a glider that he had designed and built himself. Loving also operated his own flight school and enjoyed a long and distinguished career as an aerospace research engineer.

While Loving and his story are unique, he shares with the other African-American aviation pioneers the qualities of dogged persistence and sheer love of flying that lifted them above the discrimination they faced and enabled these "Black Eagles" to soar.

BIBLIOGRAPHY

BOOKS

Briggs, Carol S. *At the Controls: Women in Aviation*. Minneapolis: Lerner Publications Company, 1991.

Davis, Benjamin O. Davis, Jr. *Benjamin O. Davis, Jr., American*. Washington, DC: Smithsonian Institution Press, 1991.

Francis, Charles E. *The Tuskegee Airmen*. Boston: Branden Publishing Company, 1988.

Hardesty, Von, and Dominick Pisano. *Black Wings: The American Black in Aviation*. Washington, DC: National Air and Space Museum, Smithsonian Institution, 1983.

Hart, Philip S. *Flying Free: America's First Black Aviators*. Minneapolis: Lerner Publications Company, 1992.

Haskins, Jim. "Ronald McNair," *One More River to Cross: The Stories of Twelve Black Americans*. New York: Scholastic Inc., 1992, pp. 182–200.

Haskins, Jim, and Kathleen Benson. *Space Challenger: The Story of Guion Bluford*. Minneapolis: Carolrhoda Books, Inc., 1984.

Loving, Neal. *Loving's Love: A Black American's Experience in Aviation*. Washington, DC: Smithsonian Institution Press, 1994.

BIBLIOGRAPHY

Rich, Doris L. *Queen Bess, Daredevil Aviator*. Washington, DC: Smithsonian Institution Press, 1993.

Sandler, Stanley. *Segregated Skies: All-Black Combat Squadrons of World War II*. Washington, DC: Smithsonian Institution Press, 1992.

ARTICLES

" 'Atlantis' Flies Atmospheric Mission," *Facts on File*, April 2, 1992.

"Blacks in Aviation History," *Ebony*, February 1994, pp. 118+.

Eugene Bullard obituary, *The New York Times*, October 14, 1961, p. 23.

Farrar, G. W., "Military Women: First Black Female Aviator: Brenda Robinson," *The Black Collegian*, April/May 1981, pp. 94–95.

"For a Black Woman, Space Isn't the Final Frontier," *The New York Times*, March 3, 1993, p. B13.

Jahn, Ed, "Tuskegee Airmen Claim Their Place in History," *The San Diego Union-Tribune*, August 2, 1992, p. B2.

Marshall, Marilyn, "Child of the '60s Set to Become First Black Woman in Space," *Ebony*, August 1989, pp. 51–52+.

"Seeking 'Fair Deal' for a Black Cadet," *The New York Times*, January 31, 1994, p. 1.

"Shuttle 'Atlantis' Launches Missile Probe," *Facts on File*, December 5, 1991, p. 917.

"U.S. 'Endeavor' Flies Science Mission," *Facts on File*, September 24, 1992, p. 713.

CHRONOLOGY

1903
Wilbur and Orville Wright succeed in keeping a manned aircraft in the air over Kitty Hawk, North Carolina, for twelve seconds.

1911
Harriet Quimby becomes the first American woman to earn a pilot's license (from the International Aviation Federation in France).

1912
Harriet Quimby dies when her plane crashes into Dorchester Bay in Boston.

1914
World War I breaks out in Europe.

1917
The United States enters World War I.

The United States Army Air Force is founded.

Eugene Bullard receives the highest French honors for his service in the Lafayette Escadrille.

1921
Bessie Coleman receives her pilot's license from the International Aviation Federation in France, the first African-American woman to do so.

Hubert Fauntleroy Julian arrives in New York City and soon becomes well known as the Black Eagle.

CHRONOLOGY

1926
The United States Department of Commerce introduces the nation's first aviation licensing laws. James Herbert Banning becomes the first African-American pilot to be licensed in America.

Bessie Coleman dies when she tumbles from an out-of-control plane in Jacksonville, Florida.

The Flying Ace, the first all-black film about flying, is released.

1927
Charles Lindbergh makes the first transatlantic flight, from New York to Paris.

1928
Amelia Earhart becomes the first woman to make a solo flight across the Atlantic.

1929
William J. Powell opens the Bessie Coleman Aero Club in Chicago.

1932
James Herbert Banning and Thomas C. Allen are the first African Americans to make a transcontinental flight.

1933
C. Alfred Anderson and Dr. Albert E. Forsythe are the first black aviators to successfully complete a transcontinental flight from Atlantic City, New Jersey, to Los Angeles, California, and back.

1934
Anderson and Forsythe attempt the South-American Goodwill flight to the Caribbean, but are unable to make the return journey.

CHRONOLOGY

William J. Powell self-publishes his autobiography, entitled *Black Wings*.

1939

World War II begins in Europe.

The Civilian Pilot's Training program is opened to blacks; Tuskegee Institute establishes a Division of Aeronautics to train black pilots under the CPT program. C. Alfred Anderson is hired as chief primary flight instructor.

1940

President Franklin D. Roosevelt issues a directive to the War Department to create a black flying unit. The Army establishes a base at Tuskegee Institute, Tuskegee Army Air Field. The training program inaugurated there becomes known as the Tuskegee Experiment.

Colonel Benjamin O. Davis, Jr., is chosen to command the new black flying unit at Tuskegee.

1941

The United States enters World War II on both the European and Pacific fronts after Japan bombs the United States naval base at Pearl Harbor in Hawaii.

The Civilian Pilots Training program is renamed the War Training Service program (WTS).

1943

The 99th Fighter Squadron, trained at Tuskegee, embarks for North Africa.

1944

The 332nd Fighter Group leaves for Italy.

CHRONOLOGY

1945

Members of the 477th Bombardment Group protest segregated officers' clubs at Godman Army Air Field, Indiana, and are arrested. An official investigation concludes that the base command had gone against Army Air Forces' regulations. Only one officer is found guilty and assessed a small fine.

The war in Europe formally ends.

Benjamin O. Davis, Jr., receives the Distinguished Flying Cross.

The war in the Pacific ends with the United States atomic bombing of Hiroshima and Nagasaki in Japan.

1947

The United States officially recognizes the importance of aviation in the military by making the Army Air Forces an independent service called the United States Air Force.

President Harry S. Truman issues Executive Order No. 9981, ordering equality of treatment and opportunity in the armed forces and establishing the President's Committee on Equality of Treatment and Opportunity in the Armed Forces.

1948

James O. Plinton, Jr., and Maurice DeYoung found Quisqueya, Ltd., a Caribbean airline that operates between Haiti and the Turks and Caicos Islands.

1950–1953

The Korean War, in which many African-American flyers, including Daniel "Chappie" James, distinguish themselves.

CHRONOLOGY

Ensign Jesse L. Brown becomes the first black naval aviator. His plane is struck as he flies a support mission in the Korean War, and Ensign Brown dies. Posthumously, he is awarded the Distinguished Flying Cross, Air Medal, and Purple Heart.

1954
Benjamin O. Davis, Sr., becomes a brigadier general.

1954–1973
The Vietnam War.

1955–1965
The direct-action civil rights movement.

1956
Perry H. Young, formerly a flight instructor at Tuskegee, is hired as a pilot for the New York Airways helicopter company.

1957
James O. Plinton joins Trans World Airlines as one of the few blacks to hold an executive position with a major commercial airline.

The world enters the space age when the Soviet Union launches *Sputnik 1*, the first unmanned spacecraft.

1963
Captain Edward Dwight is the first African American accepted into the U.S. manned space flight program; he later resigns under pressure.

1967
Air Force Major Robert H. Lawrence, Jr., is selected for the astronaut program; he dies in an airplane accident later that year.

CHRONOLOGY

1965
General Benjamin O. Davis, Jr., named Chief of Staff, United Nations Command, the second highest position in the U.N. military.

After a long court battle, Marlon D. Green wins his suit against Continental Airlines and joins the company as a pilot.

1972
U.S. Army helicopter pilot Captain Ronald A. Radcliffe, who served heroically in the war in Vietnam, is named Army Aviator of the Year.

1973
An escort ship is named in honor of Ensign Jesse L. Brown.

1974
Captain Lloyd Newton is the first black pilot to join the elite USAF Demonstration Squadron, the Thunderbirds.

1975
Daniel "Chappie" James becomes America's first black four-star general and is named Commander in Chief of the North American Air Defense Command.

1977
A Bessie Coleman Aviator's Club is founded in Chicago.

1978
Guion Bluford and two other blacks are accepted into the space shuttle program, as is the first woman, Sally Ride.

1980
A road at Chicago's O'Hare Airport is renamed Bessie Coleman Drive.

CHRONOLOGY

1983
Dr. Sally K. Ride becomes the first American woman in space.

Dr. Guion S. Bluford becomes the first African American in space.

1986
Dr. Ronald K. McNair is the first African-American astronaut to die in space when the space shuttle *Challenger* blows up as it takes off on its fifth mission.

1991
Air Force Colonel Frederick D. Gregory becomes the first African-American Mission Commander when the shuttle *Discovery* undertakes its tenth mission.

1992
Dr. Mae C. Jemison is the first African-American woman in space.

Chicago celebrates its first "Bessie Coleman Day" and, in New York, Coleman is inducted into the International Women's Sports Hall of Fame as a "pioneer."

INDEX

INDEX

INDEX

189

INDEX

INDEX

INDEX

INDEX

INDEX

INDEX

INDEX

PHOTO CREDITS